"Chinese Sentence Builders
A Lexicogrammar approach"
Beginner – Pre-intermediate

Answer Book

This is the answer booklet for "Chinese Sentence Builders – A Lexicogrammar approach. Beginner – Pre-intermediate".

It contains answers for all exercises and follows the exact order of the original book. To further make this book user-friendly there is a reference to which page a particular page relates to in the original – student book, at the start of each unit section.

We hope that you enjoy using it and that your students enjoy working with "Chinese Sentence Builders – A Lexicogrammar approach".

Thanks,

Gianfranco Conti, Dylan Viñales, Chris Webster and Maggie Sproule

Copyright © G. Conti & D. Viñales

All rights reserved
ISBN: 9798532441798

Imprint: Independently Published

Edited by Tingting Yin and Mengru Xie

TABLE OF CONTENTS

Unit 1 - Talking about my age

Unit 1. Talking about my age: VOCABULARY BUILDING (Page 6-7)

1. Match up

一岁 – **one year**　两岁 – **two years**　三岁 – **three years**　四岁 – **four years**

五岁 – **five years**　六岁 – **six years**　七岁 – **seven years**　八岁 – **eight years**

九岁 – **nine years**　十岁 – **ten years**　十一岁 – **eleven years**

十二岁 – **twelve years**

2. Complete with the missing word

a. 我**十一**岁。　b. 我哥哥**五岁**。　c. 他**叫** Robert。

d. 我哥哥**十二**岁。　e. 我姐姐**十六**岁。　f. 她**叫** Yang。她**八**岁。

3. Translate into English

a. I'm three years old　b. I'm five years old　c. I'm two years old　d. He is fifteen years old

e. She is thirteen years old　f. He is sixteen years old　g. My big brother　h. My big sister　i. She is called

4. Character Jumble

a. 我叫 An　**b.** 她叫 Yang　**c.** 我姐姐叫　**d.** 我哥哥　**e.** 十六岁　**f.** 十三岁

5. Rank the people below from oldest to youngest as shown in the example　　1, 3, 7, 6, 8, 5, 2, 4

6. For each pair of people write who is the oldest, as shown in the example　　(e.g.) B – B – B – A – A – B – A

Unit 1. Talking about my age: READING (Page 8)

1. Highlight the Chinese for the following items in Nick's text

a. 我是英格兰人　b. 我叫　c. 她叫　d. 十岁　e. 十四岁　f. 姐姐

2. Answer the following questions about Ahmed

a. Scotland　b. Twelve years old　c. 2　d. Aisha is fifteen years old and Amir is fourteen years old

3. Complete the table below

Marco, age 13, 1 sibling, age 15

Yang, age 10, 2 siblings, age 14

Ahmed, age 12, 2 siblings, ages 14 & 15

4. Claire, Yang or Marco?

a. Claire　b. Claire　c. Yang　d. Marco　e. Yang

Unit 1. Talking about my age: TRANSLATION (Page 9)

1. Faulty translation: spot and correct (in the English) any translation mistakes you find below

a. **I'm called** Patricia　b. **Two** years old　c. My **big sister** is called Martha　d. My **brother** is 5　e. I am **fifteen**

1

f. My brother is **eight**. g. My **sister**   h. **She is** 16   i. I am **19** years old   j. **He** is called John

2. From Chinese to English

a. My brother is called Raj   b. I am fifteen years old   c. My brother is sixteen years old

d. My sister is called Li Na   e. I am seven years old   f. My name is Ling Ling

g. My sister is fourteen years old   h. He is English   i. Anthony is nine years old

j. Ariana is ten years old

3. Write out the sentences

a. 我叫 Paul，我八岁。   b. 他哥哥十四岁。   c. 她叫 Li Li。她九岁。

Unit 1. Talking about my age: WRITING (Page 10)

1. Broken Pinyin

a. wǒ jiào Nassim.   b. tā shí wǔ suì.   c. wǒ jiě jie jiào Ariana.   d. tā gē ge jiào Ahmed.

2. Write out the number in Chinese

a. fourteen – 十四   b. sixteen – 十六   c. thirteen – 十三   d. seventeen – 十七

3. Spot and correct the character mistakes

a. 我叫   b. 我十岁。   c. 姐姐十五岁。   d. 我姐姐叫 Jessica。   e. 他叫 Jack。

4. Complete each gap with a suitable Chinese character

a. 我姐姐叫 Isabella。   b. 我姐姐/哥哥十五岁。   c. 他十八岁。

d. 姐姐十九岁。   e. 我/他/她十三岁。

f. 我哥哥叫 Ewan。

5. Guided writing – write 4 short paragraphs in the first person singular ['I'] each describing the people below

Samuel: 我叫 Samuel，我七岁。我哥哥叫 James，他九岁。我姐姐叫 Anna, 她八岁。

Rebecca: 我叫 Rebecca，十五岁。我哥哥叫 Jamie，他十七岁。我姐姐叫 Vicky, 她十八岁

Marco: 你好！我叫 Marco。我十一岁。我哥哥叫 Paolo，他十五岁。我姐姐叫 Gina, 她十二岁。

Ling Ling: 我叫 Ling Ling。我八岁。我哥哥叫 Ya Lun，他九岁。我姐姐叫 Li Na, 她十岁。

6. Describe this person in the third person

她叫 Jun Ming，她十五岁。

她哥哥叫 An Ping，他十九岁。

她姐姐叫 An，她十六岁。

Unit 2 - Saying when my birthday is

Unit 2. Saying when my birthday is: VOCABULARY BUILDING (Page 15)

1. Complete with the missing word

a. 我**叫** Jamie。　b. 我的**朋友**叫 Maria。　c. 我的**生日是**... 　d. 五月五日

2. Match up

一月 – **January**　二月 – **February**　四月– **April**　五月 – **May**　十一月 – **November**

十二月 – **December**　我的生日是 – **My birthday is**　我的朋友 – **my friend**　我叫 – **I am called**

他叫 – **he is called**　她叫 – **she is called**　他的 – **his**　她的 – **her**

3. Translate into English

a.14th January　b. 8th May　c. 7th February　d. 19th August　e. 25th July

4. Add the missing character

a. 生日　b. 三月　c. 朋友

5. Write out the sentence

我的生日是十二月九日

Unit 2. Saying when my birthday is: READING (Page 16)

1. Highlight the Chinese for the following items in Mei's text

a. 我叫　b. 我十二岁　c. 我是中国人　d. 我的生日是　e. 十二日　f. 她的生日是

g. 中国功夫　h. 我的朋友　i. 五月二十八日　j. 她三十五岁　k. 六月二十一日　l.哥哥

m. 一月八日

2. Complete with the missing words

我叫 Anne。**我**十三岁。我**是**英国人。我的生日是十月二十九号。我哥哥十七**岁**。他也是我的朋

友。

3. Answer the following questions about Imogen's text

a. 7　b. British　c. 5th December　d. Two brothers　e. Julian　f. 13　g. 5th December

4. Find Someone Who

a. Imogen　b. Yalun　c. Imogen　d. Yalun　e. Mei　f. Julian　g. Antonio　h. Imogen

Unit 2. Saying when my birthday is: WRITING (Page 17)

1. Complete with the missing letters

a. 我**叫** Teddy。　　b. 我是中**国**人。　　c. 她**的**生日是六月九日　d. 我的**朋友**叫 Katharine。

e. **你**是我的朋友。

2. Spot and correct the character mistakes

a. 我的生日是四月一日。　b. **他**叫 Paul。　c. 我是英国**人**。　d. 她的朋**友**叫 Caroline。　e.

Caroline **十一岁**。

3. Answer the questions in Chinese (personal answers)

a. 我叫 Chris。　 b. 我十二岁。　 c. 我的生日是十二月九日。　 d. 我是英国人。

4. Write out the dates below in words as shown in the example

a. 五月十五日　b. 六月十日　c. 三月二十日　d. 二月十九日　e. 十月二十五日

f. 一月一日　g. 十一月二十二日　h. 十二月十四日　i. 二月十六日

5. Guided writing – write 4 short paragraphs in the 1st person singular ['I'] describing the people below

小龙: 我叫小龙。我是中国人。我十一岁。我的生日是十二月二十五日。我哥哥叫大龙。他的生日是二月十九日。

Raj: 我叫 Raj。我是英国人。我十四岁。我的生日是七月二十一日。我哥哥叫 Mo。他的生日是四月二十一日。

Andrea: 我叫 Andrea。我是英国人。我十二岁。我的生日是一月一日。我哥哥叫 Paolo。他的生日是六月二十日。

Tina: 我叫 Tina。我是中国人。我十六岁。我的生日是十一日二日。我哥哥叫 Tim。他的生日是十月十二日。

6. Describe this person in the third person

她叫 Amy。她十二岁。她是中国人。她的生日是六月二十一日。她哥哥叫 Jerry。他十六岁。他的生日是十二月一日。

UNIT 2. Saying when my birthday is: TRANSLATION (Page 18)

1. Faulty translation: spot and correct (in the English) any translation mistakes you find below

a. **他**的生日是四月二十**七**日　 b. 我叫 Robert，我是**英国人**　 c. 我二十二岁

d. **他**的朋友叫 Jordan　 e. **她二十六岁**　 f. 我的生日是四月十四日

2. From Chinese to English

a. 8th October　 b. My birthday is　 c. My friend is called　 d. His birthday is　 e. 1st January

f. 14th February　 g. 25th December　 h. 8th July

3. Phrase-level translation

a. 我叫　b. 我十岁　c. 我的生日是　 d. 五月七日　 e. 她叫 Jenny

f. 我的朋友十二岁　g. 她的生日是　h. 八月二十三日　i. 四月二十九日

4. Sentence-level translation

a. 我叫 Dylan。我三十岁。我的生日是三月十一日。

b. 我哥哥叫 Peter。他十四岁。他的生日是八月十八日。

c. 我的朋友叫 John。他二十二岁。他的生日是一月十四日。

d. 我的朋友叫 Priti。她十八岁。她的生日是七月二十五日。

e. 我的朋友叫 Mei。她二十岁。她的生日是九月二十四日。

Unit 3 - Describing hair and eyes

UNIT 3. Describing hair and eyes: VOCABULARY BUILDING (Page 23)

1. Complete with the missing word

a. 黑色 b. 头发 c. 有 d. 没 and 头 e. 白

2. Match up

棕色的头发 - **brown hair** 生日 - **birthday** 金色的头发 - **blond hair** 头发 - **hair**

绿眼睛 - **green eyes** 红头发 - **red hair** 有 - have 朋友 - **friend** 黑色的头发 - **black hair**

3. Translate into English

a. blonde hair b. blue eyes c. my birthday is d. my friend is called e. December f. don't have red hair g. black hair h. she doesn't have green hair

4. Add the missing pinyin with correct tone marks

a. tā b. yǒu c. méi yǒu d. hóng sè e. lán sè f. zōng sè g. hēi h. bái

5. Broken pinyin

a. wǒ / yǒu / hóng / tóu fa b. wǒ / de / péng yǒu c. wǒ / yǒu / hēi / tóu fa

d. tā / jiào / Joe e. wǒ / yǒu / zōng sè / de / yǎn jīng f. tā / yǒu / jīn sè / de / tóu fa

g. wǒ / shí bā / suì h. tā / jiào / Maria

6. Complete with a suitable word

a. 我叫Kamala。我十岁。 b. 我有绿眼睛。 c. 我的朋友叫Jill。 d. 我有黑色的头发。

UNIT 3. Describing hair and eyes: READING (Page 24)

1. Highlight the Chinese for the following items in Misha's text

a. 我叫 b. 我哥哥 c. 他有 d. 我的生日是 e. 十日 f. 我有 g. 棕色 h. 黑色 i. 眼睛

2. Answer the following questions about Isla's text

a. 15 years old b. British c. blonde d. blue e. big sister f. green g. Isla

3. Complete with the missing words

我叫小月。我十三岁。我的生日是四月八日。我有黑头发。我有绿眼睛。我没有姐姐。

4. Answer the questions below about all five texts

a. Agnes b. Agnes c. Agnes d. Three people e. Lin jie f. Agnes g. Pablo

h. Lin Wei (Lin Jie's big brother)

UNIT 3. Describing hair and eyes: TRANSLATION (Page 25)

1. Faulty translation: spot and correct (in the English) any translation mistakes you find below

a. I have **green** eyes b. She **doesn't have** brown eyes c. **Her friend** is twelve years old

d. **She** is called Helen e. **My friend** has black hair f. I have **blue** eyes

g. **My older sister doesn't have** blue eyes h. She has **red** hair i. I have **green** hair

f. He has **white** hair

2. From Chinese to English

a. I have brown hair   b. I have black eyes   c. I don't have hair   d. He is Chinese

e. I have blond(e) hair   f. My friend is called Adam   g. She is called Misha, she is 16 years old

h. He has white hair, blue eyes   i. My older brother is 13 years old, he has blue eyes

j. Her older sister's birthday is 30th November   k. My older sister has brown hair.

3. Phrase-level translation

a. 白色的头发 b. 我叫 c. 我没有 d. 红色的头发 e. 没有头发 f. 他有 g. 十岁

h. 我有黑色的眼睛 i. 我九岁 j. 我的朋友 k. 棕色的头发 l. 金色的头发

4. Sentence-level translation

a. 我叫 Mark。我十岁。我有黑色的头发。

b. 我十二岁。我有蓝色的眼睛。我哥哥有红色的头发。

c. 我叫 Anna。我有金色的头发。

d. 我叫 Mei Ling。我的生日是六月四日。

e. 我十五岁。我有红色的头发。我的朋友有黑色的眼睛。

f. 我十三岁。我有金色的头发。我的朋友叫 Maya。

g. 她十六岁。她有棕色的头发。

UNIT 3. Describing hair and eyes: WRITING (Page 26)

1. Split sentences

a. 我有棕色的头发 b. 我的朋友是中国人 c. 我有绿眼睛 d. 我十四岁 e. 我有金色的头发

f. 我叫 Marta g. 我的生日是十月二日

2. Rewrite the sentences into the correct order

a. 我有黑色的头发。   b. 我姐姐十五岁。   c. 我叫 Patrick。   d. 我有红色的头发。

e. 他哥哥叫 Richard。   f. 我有蓝色的眼睛。

3. Spot and correct the grammar and character errors

a. 我**有**黑眼睛 b. 我哥哥**叫** Rory c. 我有白头**发** d. 他叫 Marta e. 我十四岁 f. 我**没**有头发

g. 我有绿眼睛 h. 我**有**黑色的眼睛 i. 我的生日是**一月一日** j. 我有**蓝**眼**睛**

4. Spot and correct the errors

a. 蓝**色** b. **没**有 c. 头**发** d. **红色** e. 生**日** f. 十**四** g. 我**的**朋友

5. Guided writing – write 4 short paragraphs in the first person singular ['I'] each describing the people below

Laura: 我叫 Laura。我十二岁。我有红色的头发，棕色的眼睛。我没有姐姐。我的生日是四月八日。

Anna: 我叫 Anna。我十一岁。我有金色的头发，蓝色的眼睛。我没有姐姐。我的生日是三月十三日。

Layla: 我叫 Layla。我十岁。我有棕色的头发，黑色的眼睛。我有姐姐。我的生日是五月十六日。

6. Describe this person in the third person

他叫 Joshua。他十五岁。他有红色的头发，黑色的眼睛。他有哥哥，没有姐姐。他的生日是十月十三日。

Unit 4 - Talking about my family members, saying their age and how well I get along with them. Counting to 100.

Revision Quickie 1: Numbers 1-100 / Dates / Birthdays / Hair and Eyes / Family

UNIT 4. Talking about my family + Counting to 100: VOCAB BUILDING (Page 31)

1. Complete with the missing word

a. 我家有五**个**人。　b. 我有两**个**弟弟。　c. 我的爷**爷**八十**岁**。　d. 我**和**哥哥关系好。

e. 我**妈妈**叫 Hui。

2. Match up

十六 – **16**　十二 – **12**　二十一 – **21**　一百 – **100**　三十三 – **33**　十三 – **13**　四十八 – **48**

五十二 – **52**　十五 – **15**

3. Translate into English

a. There are four people in my family　b. Me and my little sister do not have a good relationship

c. She is my grandma　d. I have two little brothers　e. Dad and grandma　f. Big sister and little brother do not have a good relationship　g. My grandpa　h. He is 24 years old

4. Add the missing letter and tones

a. jiā　b. yǒu　c. rén　d. liǎng　e. guān xi　f. nǎi nai　g. hǎo　h. mā ma

5. Broken pinyin

a. wǒ jiā / yǒu / liù / gè / rén　b. wǒ / mèi mei / shí èr / suì　c. wǒ jiā / yǒu　d. wǒ / dì di / jiào

e. wǒ / bà ba / wǔ shí wǔ / suì　f. wǒ / hé / gē ge / guān xi / bù hǎo　g. wǒ / hé / dì di / guān xi / hǎo

6. Complete with a suitable character

a. 我家有三**个**人。　b. 我有两**个**姐姐。　c. 我**和**爷爷关系好。　d. 我和他关系**不**好。

Unit 4. Talking about my family + Counting to 100: VOCABULARY DRILLS (Page 32)

1. Match up

有 – **have**　家 – **family**　关系 – **relationship**　六十 – **sixty**　妈妈 – **mother**　和 – **and**

2. Complete with the missing word

a. 我家**有**五**个**人。　b. 我**和**妈妈关系**好**。　c. **他**十七**岁**。　d. 我奶奶**八**十岁。

3. Translate into English

a. He is ninety-nine years old.　b. She is one hundred years old.　c. My dad is fifty-four years old.

d. I don't get along with my grandpa.　e. I get along with my grandma.

f. There are eight people in my family.　g. I have a little brother and two younger sisters.

1. Complete with the missing characters

a. 我家有**两个**哥哥。   b. 我家**有**三**个**人。   c. 我**奶奶**八十**一岁**。   d. 我**和**弟弟关系**不**好。

e. 我**妹妹**的生日**是**六月一日。   f. 我**妈妈**有黑色**的**头发。

5. Translate into Chinese

a. 两个姐姐 b. 妈妈和我 c. 我爸爸… d. 四十岁 e. 他的生日是八月一日 f. 我和妈妈

6. Spot and correct the errors

a. 我家~~月~~**有**三个人。   b. 我~~乃乃是~~**奶奶**八十八岁。   c. 我~~禾~~**和**姐姐关系好。

d. ~~找我~~弟~~第~~**弟**叫 Kai Nuo。

UNIT 4. Talking about my family + Counting to 100: TRANSLATION (Page 33)

1. Match up

十 – 10   二十 – 20   三十 – 30   四十 – 40   五十 – 50   六十 – 60   七十 – 70   八十 – 80   九十 – 90

一百岁 – 100

2. Write out in pinyin

a. sān shí wǔ   b. liù shí sān   c. bā shí jiǔ   d. qī shí sì   e. jiǔ shí bā   f. yì bǎi   g. bā shí èr

3. Write in the missing number

a. 我三**十**一岁。   b. 爸爸**五十七**岁。   c. 我妈妈四**十八**岁。   d. 我爷爷**一百**岁。

e. 他们**九十**岁。   f. 我爸爸的朋友**五**十岁。   g. 他**七十**岁。

4. Correct the Chinese translation errors

a. 我爸爸**十四**岁。   b. 我妈妈**四十二**岁。   c. 爸爸妈妈**四十三**岁。 d. 我**四十一**岁。

e. 她**爷爷**八十**五**岁。   f. 我**奶奶一百**岁。

5. Translate into English

a. There are six people in my family.   b. My mum is called Su Shan. She is forty-three years old.

c. My dad is called Kai. He is forty-eight years old.

d. My big sister is called An Hua. She is thirty-one years old.

e. My little sister is called An Hui. She is eighteen years old.

f. My grandfather is called An Dong. He is one hundred years old.

UNIT 4. Talking about my family + Counting to 100: WRITING (Page 34)

1. Spot and correct the mistakes

a. 四十   b. 三**十**一   c. **八**十二   d. 二**十**二   e. 十六   f. **二**十

2. Rewrite the characters so they include their missing radicals

a. 爸爸   b. 和   c. 他   d. 妹妹

3. Rewrite the sentences in the correct order

a. 我家有四个人。   b. 我和哥哥关系不好。   c. 我爸爸是中国人。 d. 我家有三个人，爸爸、妈妈和我。   e. 我爷爷叫文山，他九十三岁。

4. Gap fill

a. <u>我</u>家<u>有</u> b. <u>两个</u>姐姐 c. 她<u>叫</u> d. <u>五十岁</u> e. 他六<u>十岁</u>

5. Write a relationship sentence for each person as shown in the example

Selim: 我爸爸叫 Selim，他五十九岁，我和他关系好。

Nikita: 我妈妈叫 Nikita，她五十五岁，我和她关系不好。

Rhianna: 我姐姐叫 Rhianna，她二十八岁，我和她关系好。

Grant: 我哥哥叫 Grant，他三十六岁，我和他关系不好。

Adam: 我爷爷叫 Adam，他七十五岁，我和他关系好。

Dylan: 我爷爷叫 Dylan，他一百岁，我和他关系好。

Revision Quickie 1: Numbers 1-100, dates and birthdays, hair and eyes, family (Page 35)

1. Match

13 – 十三 14 – 十四 15 – 十五 16 – 十六 17 – 十七 18 – 十八 19 – 十九 20 – 二十

2. Translate the dates into English

a. 30th June b. 1st July c. 15th September d. 22nd March e. 31st December f. 5th January g. 30th of June h. 29th February i. 2nd December j. 17th May k. 13th September l. 8th February

3. Complete with the missing words

a. 我的生日<u>是</u>四月十五日。 b. 我十四<u>岁</u>。 c. 我哥哥有<u>黑色的</u>头发。 d. 我是中国<u>人</u>。

e. 我家有六<u>个</u>人。

4. Write out the solution in words as shown in the example

a. 十 b. 四十 c. 七十 d. 四十 e. 六十 f. 四十 g. 九十 h. 八十八 i. 五十 j. 六十三 j. 十五

5. Complete the words

a. 爷爷 b. 睛 c. 色 d. 姐姐 e. 她

6. Translate into English

a. My mother has brown eyes. b. I have blue eyes. c. My grandma is ninety years old. d. My dad's birthday is 1st of January. e. I don't have hair. f. My big sister has brown hair. g. He doesn't have green eyes. h. He has red hair.

Unit 5 - Saying where I live and am from

Grammar Time 1: Numbers 11-99, "Special Two" 两, Days of the Week

Grammar Time 2: Basic word order

UNIT 5. Saying where I live and am from: VOCAB BUILDING (Page 40)

1. Complete with the missing word

a. 我**住**在英国的北部。　　b. 她住在**中国**的南部。　　c. 他住在澳大利亚的**西**部。

d. 她住**在**南非的中部。

2. Match up

中部 – **the centre**　东部 – **the east**　南部 – **the south**　西部 – **the west**　北部 – **the north**

中国 – **China**　英国 – **the UK**　他不是 – **he is not**　我是 – **I am**　我住在 – **I live in**

3. Translate into English

a. I am Chinese　b. He isn't British　c. Dad is Taiwanese　d. I am Australian

e. He lives in the centre of South Africa　f. My big sister lives in the east of the US

g. He is called Phillippe. He is French.　h. She is called Mei. She isn't Hong Kongese.

4. Add the missing tone marks

a. táiwān　b. yīngguó　c. wǒ shì　d. tā bú shì　e. běibù　f. zhōngguó　g. wǒ zhù zài　h. měiguó

i. sūgélán　j. àodàlìyà

5. Broken pinyin

a. wǒ / zhù / zài / zhōngguó　b. tā / bú / shì / yīngguórén　c. nánfēi / de / dōngbù

d. tā / shì / xiāng gǎng / rén　e. àodàlìyà / de / nán bù

6. Complete with a suitable character

a. 她**住**在新加坡。　　b. 他住在英**国**的南部。　　c. 你住**在**香港的北部。　　d. 妈妈不是**美**国人。

e. 爷爷是**南**非人。

Unit 5. "Geography test". Match the numbers to the places on the map (Page 41)

中国：1 – 北京　2 – 上海　3 – 香港　4 – 昆明　5 – 成都

South East Asia (东南亚) / Oceania:　1 – 台湾　2 – 新加坡　3 – 印度尼西亚　4 – 马来西亚

5 – 澳大利亚

UNIT 5. Saying where I live and am from: READING (Page 42)

1. Highlight the Chinese for the following in Isabella's text

a. 我叫　b. 我二十一岁　c. 我是香港人　d. 我和我的好朋友　e. 中国的东部　f. 他是上海人

g. 他的生日是七月十日　h. 黑色的头发　i. 六月　j. 关系　k. 他的眼睛

2. Complete the statements below based on Carl's text

a. I am **22** years old   b. My birthday is the **9**[th] of **August**   c. I live in a **south** of Scotland   d. Edward is a very **good** person   e. I have a **friend** called Li   f. Li is **Chinese**   g. He lives in the north of **China**

3. Answer the questions on the four texts above

a. 15   b. Ron   c. Carl   d. Isabella   e. Isabella   f. Steph

g. Isabella   h. Steph   i. Steph's friend

4. Correct any incorrect statements about Steph's text

a. Steph 住在澳大利亚的**南**部。   b. 她的朋友住在澳大利亚的东部。 **CORRECT**

c. 她的生日是**五**月九号。   d. 她的朋友有**红**色的头发。   e. Steph 十九岁。

g. 她是澳大利亚人。 **CORRECT**

UNIT 5. Saying where I live and am from: TRANSLATION/WRITING (Page 43)

1. Translate into English

a. I live in   b. I am   c. Chinese   d. Singapore   e. Taiwanese   f. Central Scotland

g. She is not French   h. I live in the west part of South Africa   i. He lives in Hong Kong

j. My friend lives in the US   k. She isn't Irish   l. Northern Ireland   m. She is Welsh

2. Gapped sentences

a. 他住在中国的**北部** b. 我**有**一个好朋友   c. 她**是**英国人

3. Complete the sentences with a suitable character

a. 他住在英**国**。   b. 她住在**南**非。   c. 我姐姐是香港**人**。   d. 她住在爱尔兰的西**部**。

4. Phrase-level translation (English to Chinese)

a. 我住在   b. 我是   c. 中国人   d. 南部   e. 西部   f. 美国   g. 英国人   h. 我没有   i. 东部   j. 我有

k. 北部

5. Sentence-level translation (English to Chinese)

a. 我叫 Jane。我是英国人，不是中国人。我住在英国的北部。我十四岁。

b. 我不是英国人，我是中国人。我住在中国的南部。我二十三岁。我妹妹叫 May。

c. 她是南非人。她住在英国的东部。她二十七岁。她的生日是四月十日。

d. 他是美国人。他住在英国。他没有弟弟。

Unit 5. Saying where I live and am from: WRITING (Page 44)

1. Complete with the missing tone marks

a. wǒ jiào Paul   b. nǎinai zhù zài měiguó de běibù   c. tā gēge shì táiwānrén

d. tā jiějie bú shì yīngguórén   e. nǐ zhù zài xiānggǎng de dōngbù

f. māma shì fǎguórén, tā zhù zài fǎguó   g. gēge sān shí suì, tāde shēngrì shì shí yī yuè bā rì

h. yéye méi yǒu hēisè de tóufa

2. Spot and correct the character mistakes

a. 我是中国**人** b. 他是苏格兰人   c. 我**哥哥**住在澳大利亚的南部   d. 她姐姐住在**英**国

e. 我有哥哥，我**没**有姐姐 f. 我**住**在英国的北部 g. 妈妈的生日是十二月三十一**日**

3. Answer the questions in Chinese (personal answers)

a. 我叫 Maggie b. 我十二岁 c. 我的生日是八月十一日 d. 我是新加坡人 e. 我住在英国

f. 我住在英国的北部

4. Character Jumble

a. 中国人 b. 台湾人 c. 香港人 d. 新加坡人 e. 澳大利人 f. 南非人 g. 英国人 h. 法国人

5. Guided writing – write 5 short paragraphs in the 1st person singular ['I'] describing the people below

Samuel: 我叫 Samuel。我十二岁。我的生日是六月二十日。我住在伦敦。我是英国人。

Jackie: 我叫 Jackie。我十四岁。我的生日是十月十四日。我住在香港。我是中国人。

Chen: 我叫 Chen。我十一岁。我的生日是一月十五日。我住在新加坡。我是新加坡人。

Li Wei: 我叫 Li Wei。我十三岁。我的生日是一月十七日。我住在台北。我是台湾人。

Nina: 我叫 Nina。我十五岁。我的生日是十月十九日。我住在北京。我是中国人。

6. Describe this person in the third person

我叫 Tingting。我十六岁。我的生日是五月十五日。我有黑色的头发，蓝色的眼睛。我是中国人。我住在英国。

Grammar Time 1: Drills (Page 45-48)

1. Translate into English

a. 31 b. 34 c. 48 d. 56 e. 79 f. 85 g. 99 h. 11 i. 19 j. 87

2. Translate into Chinese

a. 二十六 b. 三十四 c. 四十三 d. 五十六 e. 六十八 f. 七十一 g. 九十九 h. 十四 i. 八 j. 十

3. Put the numbers in the correct order as shown

a. 二十三 b. 五十四 c. 六十一 d. 三十六 e. 九十二 f. 七十五 g. 八十七 h. 二十一 i. 九十八

4. Complete with the appropriate missing character based on content learned in previous units

a. 昨天是**星**期二。 b. 今天**是**星期四。 c. 明**天**是星期六。 d. 后天是星**期一**。

e. 我的生日是今**天**。 f. 我有两**个**姐姐。 g. 我弟弟两**岁**。 h. 今天是十一月二**日**。

5. Complete with 两 or 二

a. 他有两个妹妹 b. 星期二 c. 我的生日是二月十八号 d. 妹妹两岁 e. 她的朋友十二岁 f. 爸爸的哥哥四十二岁 g. 她们有两个姐姐

6. Translate into Chinese

a. 我有两个姐姐 b. 你有两个弟弟 c. 他两岁 d. 她二十二岁 e. 星期天   f. 今天是星期二

g. 我奶奶有两个哥哥 h. 我的生日是明天 i. 我妈妈有两个妹妹 j. 星期日

7. Guided Writing

我二十岁。我有一个哥哥，他二十二岁。他有红色的头发，黑色的眼睛。我和他关系好。我有

两个妹妹，一个十二岁，一个十四岁。我爸爸妈妈有黑色的头发，棕色的眼睛。我妈妈的生日是十二月二日。

8. Write an 80 to 100 character text

1. 我爸爸叫Ken。他五十八岁。他的生日是八月二十六日。他有棕色的头发，棕色的眼睛。他是英国人。他住在英国的中部。我和他关系好。

2. 我妈妈叫Tessa。他五十五岁。他的生日是八月二十三日。她有棕色的头发，棕色的眼睛。她是英国人。她住在英国的中部。我和她关系好。

Grammar Time 2: Pronouns - Drills (Page 50)

1. Match up

我们是 – **we are**   不是 – **is not**   我是 – **I am**   你是 – **you are**   你们是 – **you guys are**

他们是 – **they are**   他是 – **he is**   她是 – **she is**   她不是 – **she is not**

2. Complete with the missing pronoun

a. **我们**是好人 b. **他们**是法国人 c. **我们**是弟弟 d. **她**是姐姐 e. **你们**是英国人

3. Translate into English

a. I am a person   b. you are not me   c. you and I are two people d. we are not them

e. he is big brother, he is little brother   f. she is my grandma, not my mum

g. he is my friend, not my dad   h. I am Chinese, not British

4. Rewrite the sentences into the correct order

a. 他们是朋友。   b. 他是我的朋友。   c. 我们不是姐妹。   d. 他们不是中国人。   e. 她是我的妈妈。   f. 我爱我的家人。

5. Translate into Chinese

a. 你是 b. 他是 c. 你们 d. 他们是 e. 我们是

3. Spot and correct the errors

a. 我是~~爹~~**爷**爷。   b. 她是~~不~~**不是**中国~~人~~人。   c. 他们~~足~~**是**~~不~~**是**中国~~人~~人。   d. 他**她**们是姐姐。

e. ~~戈~~**我**爱你。   f. 你不是~~央~~**英**国~~人~~人。

Grammar Time 2: Verb 有 (to have) – Drills (Page 52)

1. Translate into Chinese

a. 爸爸有 b. 我没有 c. 她没有 d. 他们有 e. 我们有

2. Translate into English

a. we have black hair b. she has blonde hair c. mum has white hair d. dad has brown hair

e. they have green eyes f. we don't have hair g. we have older sisters, not older brothers

h. he doesn't have hair, he has green eyes

3. Spot and correct the mistakes

a. 我妈**妈有**金头发 b. 我弟弟有**白**头发 c. 我没有头发 **CORRECT**

d. 他们有黑头发 **CORRECT**　e. 我们**没**有头发　f. 我爸爸妈妈**没**有红色的头发

4. Spot and correct the errors in the English translation

a. **Our** mother has white hair　b. **She** has green **eyes**　c. **He** has brown eyes and **black** hair

d. His **friend doesn't have blue** eyes　e. **My** friend has blond hair and **has blue** eyes

f. **Grandad doesn't have** hair

5. Translate into Chinese

a. 我们有白色的头发　b. 你没有头发　c. 你们有红色的头发　d. 她有棕色的眼睛

e. 我妈妈有妹妹　f. 我姐姐有黑色的头发　g. 我爸爸有白色的头发　h. 我爷爷没有头发

6. Rewrite the sentences into the correct order

a. 他有蓝头发　b. 我爷爷和我有白头发　c. 他们没有头发　d. 我们没有头发

Grammar Time 2: Drills (Page 53)

1. Translate into Chinese

a. 我们是英国人　b. 她们有黑色的眼睛　c. 他十一岁　d. 他们四十五岁　e. 她们是中国人　f. 她们没有棕色的头发　g. 他们没有头发

2. Complete with 没 or 不

a. 妈妈**没**有金头发。　b. 我姐姐**不**是中国人。　c. 他们**没**有绿眼睛。　d. 他们**不**是朋友。　e. 我的爸爸和爷爷**没**有头发。　f. 她是姐姐，**不**是妹妹。

3. Spot and correct the errors

a. **他**是哥哥　b. 她是哥哥，**不**是弟弟　c. 你们和我**是**朋友　d. 他们**有**红头发

e. 他的爸爸**没**有白头发　f. 我和他**不**是朋友　g. 我**和**他们**是**好朋**友**

4. Guided writing

我九岁。我有一个哥哥。我哥哥十五岁。他有棕色的头发，黑色的眼睛。他的生日是十一月三十日。我有一个姐姐。她十二岁。她有黑色的头发，棕色的眼睛。我爸爸妈妈有棕色的头发，棕色的眼睛。

5. Write an 80 to 100 words text

我有四个朋友，一个叫 Dylan。他十六岁。他的生日是三月十八日。他有黑色的头发，棕色的眼睛。他是英国人。他住在英国的中部。我和他关系好。

一个叫 Amy。她十四岁。她的生日是七月三日。她有红色的头发，蓝色的眼睛。她是美国人。她住在美国的西部。我和她关系好。

一个叫 Chang。他十五岁。他的生日是九月十二日。他有黑色的头发，黑色的眼睛。他是中国人。他住在中国的东部。我和他关系不好。

一个叫 Maggie。她十七岁。她的生日是五月三十日。她有蓝色的头发，棕色的眼睛。她是苏格兰人。她住在苏格兰的南部。我和她关系好。

七月十七日，星期四

Unit 6 – Intro to describing myself and another family member (Part 1/2)

Grammar Time 3: Ownership with 的

Grammar Time 4: Word order with 是 and 很

Unit 6. Part 1: VOCABULARY BUILDING (Page 58)

1. Match up

我很高 – **I am tall**   我很矮 – **I am short**   我很可爱 – **I am cute**

我很瘦 – **I am skinny**   我很小气 – **I am mean**   我很烦人 – **I am annoying**

我很苗条 – **I am slim**   我很友好 – **I am friendly**   我很乐观 – **I am optimistic**

2. Complete with the missing word

a. 我弟弟**很**坏。   b. 我爸爸很**友好**。   c. 我姐姐很**聪明**。   d. 他很**好看**。   e. 我哥哥**很**无聊。

3. Categories – sort the adjectives below in the categories provided

外貌: a. 美丽   b. 好看   d. 难看   e. 矮   g. 胖   h. 丑   j. 瘦   l. 漂亮

个性: c. 小气   f. 无聊   i. 好玩   k. 乐观

4. Complete the characters

a. 苗条   b. 可爱   c. 友好   d. 帅   e. 瘦

5. Translate into English

a. My older sister is mean   b. My younger brother is fat   c. My older brother is boring

d. My mother is friendly   e. I am not ugly   f. I am not bad looking   g. Her friend is pretty

h. His friend is handsome

6. Spot and correct the translation mistakes

a. ~~He is~~ **I am** slim   b. ~~He~~ **She** is ~~clever~~ **pretty**   c. I ~~am~~ **am not** ugly   d. My ~~mother~~ **little sister** is short

e. My ~~sister~~ **older brother** is ~~bad~~ **tall**

7. English to Chinese translation

a. 我很好看   b. 我妈妈很好玩   c. 我姐姐很可爱   d. 我弟弟很烦人   e. 我很友好

f. 我爸爸很高，不胖

"""

Unit 6 - Describing my family and saying why I like/dislike them (Part 2/2)

Unit 6. (Part 2) Describing my family: VOCABULARY BUILDING (Page 62)

1. Complete with the missing word

a. 我家**没**有   b. 有四**个**人   c. 我妈妈**叫**安   d. 我**和**爸爸关系好   e. 我叔叔**很**高

2. Match up

我阿姨 – **My aunt**   我爷爷 – **My grandad**   我妈妈 – **My mum**   我爸爸 – **My dad**

我哥哥 – **My big brother**   我妹妹 – **My little sister**   我弟弟 – **My little brother**

我叔叔 – **My uncle**   我奶奶 – **My grandma**

3. Translate into English

a. He is my uncle   b. My little brother is generous   c. I also like her eyes   d. Because I'm friendly

e. I get along well with big brother   f. Because we have a bad relationship

g. I like him, because he is nice   h. I'm also a little fat

4. Add the missing pinyin and tone marks

a. shuài   b. piào liang   c. hǎo kàn   d. dà fang   e. hǎo wán   f. cōng ming   g. miáo tiao   h. xiǎo qì

i. qīn qiè   j. měi

5. Broken Pinyin

a. wǒ jiā yǒu…   b. sì gè rén   c. wǒ mā ma hěn qīn qiè   d. tā men guān xi hǎo

e. wǒ shū shu hěn dà fang   f. wǒ hé tā guān xi bù hǎo

6. Complete with a suitable word

a. 我家**有**五个人。   b. 我妈妈**很**亲切。   c. 她**有**蓝眼睛。   d. 我妈妈很**可**爱。 e. 我喜**欢**他们。

f. 我弟弟有**一点**帅。

Unit 6. (Part 2) Describing my family: READING (Page 63)

1. Find the Chinese in Lun Mei's text

a. 我叫   b. 南部   c. 我有一个哥哥   d. 因为   e. 友好   f. 我爸爸   g. 棕色的眼睛   h. 头发

2. Answer the following questions about Messi's text

a. 10 years old   b. USA   c. 8 people   d. his uncle   e. because he is fun and nice/friendly

f. his aunt   g. 5th May

3. Complete with the missing words

我**叫** Ali，我九**岁**。我家有四**个**人。我**和**爷爷关系好，因为他**很**友好。我爸爸**有**白头发和绿色**的**眼睛。

4. Find someone who...

a. Huan   b. Meng   c. Messi's aunt   d. Messi   e. Lun Mei   f. Roslan   g. Meng   h. Meng's big sister

i. Messi and his aunt

Unit 6. (Part 2) Describing my family: TRANSLATION (Page 64)

1. Faulty translation: spot and correct any translation mistakes (in the English) you find below

a. In ~~my~~ **his** family ~~I have~~ **he has** four people

b. My mother is called Yen and my ~~aunt~~ **uncle** is called Zen

c. ~~My father~~ **Me** and my granny have a good relationship   d. ~~My father~~ **Their uncle** is called Ivan

e. ~~Brother~~ **Uncle** Ivan is very fun, also a little ~~skinny~~ **handsome**

f. ~~His~~ **My** uncle Zen ~~is~~ **is not** Chinese   g. ~~She lives~~ **I live** in the north of China

2. From Chinese to English

a. I like my grandad   b. My grandmother is kind   c. My uncle has blond hair   d. I get along well with my older brother

e. I get on badly with my aunt   f. I like my granddad because he is generous   g. My little sister is nice and also a little bit cute   h. I don't like my younger brother, because he is annoying

3. Phrase-level translation

a. 他很友好 b. 她很大方 c. 我和他关系好   d. 我和弟弟关系不好

e. 我叔叔很好玩，可是他有一点胖 f. 我弟弟很帅 g. 我喜欢我的阿姨 Mary，她很友好

h. 她有两个姐姐 i. 他有白头发 j. 我不喜欢我的爷爷 k. 他们很小气

4. Sentence-level translation

a. 我叫 Pei Qi。我九岁。我家有四个人。   b. 我叫 Carla。我有蓝色的眼睛。我和弟弟关系好。

c. 我和哥哥关系不好，因为他不好玩。

d. 我叫 Frank。我住在中国。我不喜欢我姐姐，因为她很小气。

e. 我很喜欢我妈妈，因为她很友好。

f. 我家有五个人。我喜欢我的爸爸，我不喜欢我的妈妈。

Unit 6. (Part 2) Describing my family: WRITING (Page 65)

1. Split sentences

我爸爸是**中国人** 我妈妈很**友好** 我有黑**色的头发** 我和他**关系好**

我不喜欢她，**因为她很小气** 我很瘦，**也有一点矮**

2. Rewrite the sentences in the correct order

a. 我家有四个人。   b. 我和弟弟关系好。   C. 我不喜欢叔叔。   D. 我妈妈有蓝色的眼睛。

e. 我姐姐很好玩。

3. Spot and correct the grammar and character errors

a.我家里**页：有** b. 我**关系好和他：和他关系好**   c. 我喜**欠我阿姨：欢**

d. 我**未未是友好：妹妹很** e. 我爸爸是大方：**很** f. 他有眼睛蓝色的：**蓝色的眼睛**

g. 我姐姐**是高：很** h. 我爷爷**头发没有：没有头发**

4. Spot and correct the errors

a. 蓝色 b. 大方 c. 小气 d. 很 e. 喜欢 f. 因为 g. 友好 h. 一点

5. Guided writing – write 3 short paragraphs describing the people below in the first person

Paco: 我叫 Paco。我十二岁。我家有四个人。我喜欢我的妈妈，她很友好。她有金色的头发。我也喜欢我的哥哥，因为他很友好。我不喜欢我的妹妹 Gemma，因为她很烦人。

Li An: 我叫 Li An。我十一岁。我家有五个人。我喜欢我的爸爸。他很胖。他有黑色的头发。我也喜欢我的奶奶，因为她很大方。我不喜欢我的爷爷 Yao，因为他很小气。

Luo Li: 我叫 Luo Li。我十岁。我家有三个人。我喜欢我的爷爷。他很高。他没有头发。我也喜欢我的妹妹，因为她很亲切，也有一点可爱。我不喜欢我的奶奶 Mi Ya，因为她很坏。

6. Describe this person in the third person:

爷爷叫 Bo lin。他有白头发和棕色的眼睛。我很喜欢他。他很高，也很帅。他很友好，也很大方。

Grammar Time 3: Ownership with 的 (Page 66)

1. Translate

a. 爸爸的　b. 朋友的　c. 哥哥的　d. 你的　e. 我们的

2. Translate into English

a. Her eyes are beautiful　b. Their big brother is smart　c. Grandad is my dad's dad

d. I call dad's mum grandmother　e. He is my dad's little brother, I call him uncle

3. Translate into Chinese

a. 他妈妈很友好。　b. 他们的姐姐是我的朋友。　c. 他们的爷爷八十九岁。他很大方。

d. 我们的弟弟很高。他很小气。　e. 我姐姐有红色的头发。她不高。

f. 她是我们的妈妈，她的眼睛很美。　g. Buzz 的朋友叫 Woody。　h. Ron 是 Hermione 的朋友。

Grammar Time 4: Word order with 是 & 很 (Page 67)

1. Translate into English

a. We are friends　b. My big sister is annoying　c. Your mum is very friendly　d. Their grandmother is cute

e. We are British　f. My friend is boring

2. Translate into Chinese

a. 他爸爸很聪明　b. 我很漂亮　c. 她们是我的姐姐　d. 我很大方

e. Freya 很友好　f. 我妈妈很高，我爸爸是法国人　g. 我奶奶很苗条，我爷爷有一点胖

3. Complete the sentence with 是 or 很

a. 我**很**聪明　b. 我爷爷和爸爸**很**矮　c. 他**是**我的朋友，他**很**高　d. 爷爷**很**乐观

e. 她**是**一个好人，也**很**亲切　f. 他们**是**中国人

Unit 7 - Talking about pets

Grammar Time 5: Saying 'also' with 也

Questions skills: Age / Descriptions / Pets

Unit 7. Talking about pets: VOCABULARY BUILDING (Page 72)

1. Complete with the missing word

a. 我家有一只**鸟**　b. 我家**没**有兔子　c. 我想要一只**狗**　d. 我想要三条**鱼**　e. 我家没有**猫**

2. Translate into English

a. At home I have a big bird, it's name is Bob　b. My friend Lina has a kitten, it's very cute

c. At home he has two snakes　d. At home I have three dogs　e. I would like to have a small rabbit

f. My big brother has a small fish

3. Add the missing pinyin with the correct tone marks

a. gǒu　b. māo　c. méi yǒu　d. zhī　e. tùzi　f. chǒngwù　g. jiā　h. tiáo

4. Broken pinyin

a. wǒ / jiā / yǒu / sān / tiáo / gǒu　b. yì zhī / dà / māo　c. tā / jiā / yǒu / sì / zhī / xiǎo / tù zi

d. wǒ / jiā / méi / yǒu / chǒng wù　e. wǒ / péng yǒu / yǒu / liǎng / tiáo / dà / shé

f. wǒ / gē **ge** / xiǎng / yào / yì / zhī / gǒu　g. wǒ / bù / xiǎng / yào / niǎo

5. Match up

一只猫 – **a cat**　一只狗 – **a dog**　两条鱼 – **two fish**　一条蛇 – **a snake**　一只鸟 – **a bird**

一只兔子 – **a rabbit**　一条大鱼 – **a big fish**　两条蛇 – **two snakes**　一只小鸟 – **a small bird**

Unit 7. Talking about pets: READING (Page 73)

1. Highlight the Chinese in 小月's text?

a. 两只宠物　b. 叫　c. 一只白猫　d. 一只黑狗　e. 帅　f. 我弟弟　g. 爸爸　h. 好玩　i. 有一点凶

j. 四个人

2. Find someone who? – answer the questions below about 小月, Roberto, Selena and Jules

a. 小月　b. Robert and Jules　c. Selena　d. Selena　e. Jules　f. 小月 and Robert

3. Answer the following questions about Jule's text

a. West of South Africa　b. Funny and kind　c. George and Michael　d. Sam is Jules's snake

e. Sam is bad and a bit ugly　f. Dennis is Jule's rabbit　g. Dennis is fat and not very clever

4. Fill in the table below

Selena: age – **20**　country – **Australia**　pets – **bird, fish**　description of pets – **they are humorous**

Robert: age – **9**　country – **UK**　pets – **dog, snake**　description of pets – **Ricky - annoying, snake - quiet**

5. Fill in the blanks (with the most appropriate word)

a. 叫　b. 岁　c. 住　d. 有　e. 只

Unit 7. Talking about pets: TRANSLATION (Page 74)

1. Faulty translation: spot and correct any translation mistakes you find below

a. In my family there are ~~four~~ five people and ~~three~~ **two** pets

b. At home we have two pets, a dog and a ~~rabbit~~ **cat**

c. My ~~brother~~ **friend** ~~has a rabbit~~ **is** called Paul. It is ~~very boring~~ **fun**

d. My big ~~sister~~ **brother** has a ~~small~~ **big** bird called Dylan

e. My ~~father~~ **mother** has a ~~fish~~ **snake.** It is called Nicole

2. Translate into English

a. An extremely cute cat   b. An very clever dog   c. A bird that is a Little bit boring

d. An extremely pretty snake   e. A fish that is quite big   f. A humourous dog

g. A big cat that is quite thin   h. Three extremely fat pets   i. At home I have five pets

j. I would like to have a small rabbit

3. Phrase-level translation (English to Chinese)

a. 一只大狗   b. 一只小猫   c. 一个人   d. 我们住在   e. 她非常漂亮/美   f. 它非常好玩   g. 我有

h. 我没有   i. 我想要   j. 她想要   k. 它有一点丑

4. Sentence-level translation (English to Chinese)

a. 我哥哥有一只白狗。它叫 Fluffy。   b. 我姐姐有一只鸟。它叫大红。它很丑。

c. 妈妈有一只猫。它叫 Gordon。它非常胖。   d. 它有一条小鱼。它叫 Tina。它有一点凶。

e. 爸爸有一只大狗。它叫 Stuart。它非常大。   f. 我有一只猫、一只狗和两只鸟。

g. 我弟弟有两条大鱼。它们叫 Nemo 和 Dory。它们很漂亮/美。

h. 我妹妹想要一只小猫。   i. 我家没有鱼。

Unit 7. Talking about pets: WRITING (Page 75)

1. Split sentences

我有一只兔子，**它叫 Speedy.** 我家有一只大**狗**   我有一只白**色的小猫**   我家有一条**蛇**

我想**要一条鱼**

2. Rewrite the sentences in the correct order

a. 我家有三只宠物。   b. 我想要一只兔子。   c. 我有一只猫和一只鸟。

d. 我的朋友有一条黑蛇。   e. Fran 家有一只白猫。   f. 我家没有狗。

3. Spot and correct the grammar and character [note: in several cases characters are missing]

a. 我家有一只鸟**和**一只猫。   b. 我家有两**条**绿蛇。   c. 我很想**要一只**鸟。

d. 我妹妹有一**只**大猫。   e. 我的朋友**有**一只大兔子。   f. 我的小**狗**叫 Terence。

4. Character Jumble

a. 我想要   b. 我家有   c. 一只狗   d. 比较胖   e. 非常大

5. Guided writing – write 3 short paragraphs (in 1ˢᵗ person) describing the pets below using the details in the box

Woof: 我叫 Woof。我四岁。我是一只黑狗。我四岁。我很可爱。

Meow: 我叫 Meow。我六岁。我是一只白猫。我很好玩。

Nemo: 我叫 Nemo。我一岁。我是一条红鱼。我很漂亮。

6. Describe this person in the third person:

他叫 Robert。我有黑色的头发，蓝色的眼睛。我很友好。我很高，也很胖。我家有一只狗、一只猫和两条鱼。我想要一只鸟。

Grammar Time 5: Saying "also" with 也 (Pets and description) (Page 76)

1. Translate into Chinese

a. 我也有　b. 你也有　c. 她也有　d. 我们也有　e. 你们也有　f. 他们也有

2. Translate into English

a. I also have a kitten, it's very cute　b. My big brother also has a puppy, but it's a little bit boring

c. My mum also has a big bird, it's very fat　d. My friend also has a snake, it's very fierce

e. At home I have a fish, it's not clever

3. Complete the sentences

a. 我**也**有一条蛇。　b. 她**也**两岁。　c. 我们**也**有一只鸟。它**也**四岁。　d. 我姐姐**也**有一只鸟。

4. Translate into Chinese

a. 我也有一条鱼。它三岁。　b. 我们也没有猫　c. 我的狗也三岁。它很大。

d. 我也想要一只狗。

Question Skills 1: Age/Descriptions/Pets (Page 77)

1. Match question and answer

你几岁？–**我十岁。**

她高吗？–**不高。**

你爸爸人怎么样？–**他很亲切，也很友好。**

你妈妈多大？–**她三十九岁。**

你喜欢什么颜色？–**红色。**

你妹妹叫什么名字？–**她叫 Eileen。**

你好吗？–**我不好。**

你家有宠物吗？–**有，一条鱼和一只鸟。**

你喜欢什么宠物？–**小猫！它们很可爱！**

你有几个宠物？–**两个。一只猫和一只狗。**

你是哪国人？–**我是英国人。**

你有兄弟姐妹吗？– **没有。**

你喜欢你哥哥吗？– **不喜欢！**

你的生日是几月几号？– **六月二十号。**

2. Complete with the missing words

a. 你是**哪**国人？　b. 他人**怎么样？**　c. 你爸爸**多大**？　d. 你妈妈好**吗**？

e. 你生日是**几月几**日？　f. 你的狗叫**什么**？　g. 你家有几**宠物**？　h. 你有几个**兄弟**？

3. Translate into Chinese

a. What are you called?　b. How old are you?　c. Is she pretty?

d. How many brothers and sisters do you have?　e. Is grandma well?

f. What's your older brother like?　g. How many pets do you have?　h. Which country are you from?

4. Translate the following question patterns into English

a. What?　b. How is it?　c. Which one?　d. How old?　e. How are you?　f. Do you like her?

g. Is he handsome?

Unit 8 - Saying what jobs people do...

Grammar Time 6: Two words for "but" [可是、但是]

Unit 8. Saying what jobs people do: VOCABULARY BUILDING (Page 85)

1. Complete with the missing word

a. 我爸爸**是**商**人**   b. 我阿姨**是**护**士**   c. 我哥哥**是**厨**师**   d. 我妈妈**是**医**生**   e. 我叔叔**是**演**员**

2. Match up

很无聊 - **it's boring**   很难 - **it's hard**   很好玩 - **it's fun**   很有压力 - **it's stressful**

因为 - because   喜欢 - like   没意思 - **it's boring**   家庭主夫 - **house husband**   很容易 - **it's easy**

3. Translate into English

a. My mum is a worker   b. I like his job   c. Work in a company   d. My big brother is an engineer

e. Boring job   f. My big sister is a nurse   g. He loves this job   h. Because it's very easy

4. Add the missing tone marks

a. gōng rén   b. **gōng sī**   c. sī jī   d. lǎo shī   e. gōng zuò   f. xué xiào   g. yǒu yì sì   h. xǐ huan

5. Character Jumble

a. 中国人   b. 星期六   c. 售货员   d. 有压力   e. 工作室   f. 英国人

6. Broken pinyin

a. wǒ / bà ba / shì / sī jī   b. tā / xǐ huān   c. wǒ / gē ge / shì / huà jiā

d. tā / zài xué xiào/ gōng zuò   e. tā/ hěn / tǎo yàn…   f. tā / zài / yī yuàn / gōng zuò

g. yīn wèi/ hěn/nán

7. Complete with a suitable word

a. 我妈妈是老**师**。   b. 你的**工作**   c. 他喜欢**这**个工作，因**为**很有意思。   d. 她在医院**工**作。

e. 她是医**生**，不是护**士**。

Unit 8. Saying what jobs people do: READING (Page 86)

1. Highlight the Chinese in Roo's text

a. 我二十岁   b. 我有一只狗   c. 四个人   d. 医生   e. 在城市   f. 他喜欢他的工作   g. 很重要

h. 可是   i. 难   j. 也很有压力

2. Answer the questions on ALL texts

a. Kinga's father   b. Ross's mum   c. Joshua's uncle   d. Roo   e. Kinga   f. Ross

3. Answer the following questions about Joshua's text

a. Hong Kong   b. His mum   c. She's a teacher. She works at home   d. He is fierce and unfriendly   e. He's a shop assistant   f. Merlin is Joshua's fish   g. Agnes is Joshua's big sister.

4. Fill in the table below

Maria: age – **27**   country – **USA**   pets/job – **one cat, teacher**   description of pets/job – pet: **beautiful** job: **important**

THE LANGUAGE GYM

Ross: age – **N/A**   country – **N/A**   pets/job – **one dog, nurse**   Description of pets/job – pet: **very big and a little bit fat** job - **interesting, very stressful**

5. Fill in the blanks

我<u>叫</u>Maria。我<u>住</u>在美国。我二十七<u>岁</u>。我有一只猫。它很美。我是老<u>师</u>，我喜欢这个<u>工</u>作，因为很重<u>要</u>。

Unit 8. Saying what jobs people do: TRANSLATION (Page 87)

1. Faulty translation: spot and correct [IN THE ENGLISH] any translation mistakes you find below

a. ~~Our father~~ **My mum** is a ~~driver~~ **chef** and ~~he~~ **she** really likes ~~his~~ **her** job because it is interesting. **She** works in a **school**.

b. ~~My aunt~~ **His big sister** works as a business person in the city. She ~~doesn't like~~ **can't stand** this job because it's ~~easy~~ **extremely difficult**.

c. ~~Her aunt~~ **My little brother** is a ~~nurse~~ **doctor**. ~~She~~ **He** works in a hospital and likes working as a ~~nurse~~ **doctor**.

d. My ~~uncle~~ **grandfather** Gianfranco is a ~~shop assistant~~ **business man**, he works in a big ~~supermarket~~ **company**. He likes this job.

e. My mum is an actress and works in ~~an office~~ **a studio**. She also works as a shop assistant on ~~Tuesdays~~ **Mondays** in a **shop**. She ~~likes~~ **dislikes** it because it is ~~important~~ **boring**.

2. Translate into English

a. My uncle works at…   b. Our mum is…   c. She works at home   d. Nurses work at hospitals

e. There are two doctors and an actor in my family   f. I am an engineer   g. She loves her job

h. I work in a studio   f. They work in a shop   g. My little brother works in a school

3. Phrase-level translation (English to Chinese)

a. 我哥哥 b. 这个工作 **c.** 两个医生 d. 他喜欢 e. 她不喜欢 f. 因为没意思 g. 很好玩

h. 非常有意思

4. Sentence-level translation (English to Chinese)

a. 我哥哥是工人。   b. 我爸爸是护士。   c. 我爷爷是医生，他爱他的工作。

d. 我哥哥在公司工作。   e. 我们有一只猫叫 Sally。   f. 我有一只友好的狗和一只很凶的猫。

g. 我妈妈是司机。她喜欢她的工作。   h. …因为很有意思。   i. 我姐姐在家工作。

Unit 8. Saying what jobs people do: WRITING (Page 88)

1. Split sentences

我哥哥有**一只白色的兔子**   我阿姨是**老师**   我叔叔在**学校工作**   她喜欢**她的工作**   因为很**有意思**
我不喜**欢这个工作**   家庭**主妇**

2. Rewrite the sentences in the correct order

a. 她非常喜欢这个工作。   b. 他们喜欢在公司工作。   c. 她是家庭主妇。

d. 我弟弟是一个司机。　　e. 我姐姐在工作室工作。　　f. 他喜欢这个工作。　　g. 医生在医院。

3. Spot and correct the grammar and characters [note: in several cases characters are missing]

a. 我妈妈**是**家庭**王妇**　b. 这个工作**很无聊**，也非常不好玩　c. 我姐姐**是**工程**帅**

d. 她很讨厌**这**个工**作**，因**为**非常难　e. 我们**在**城市工作

f. 他非常喜欢这个工作，**因为**很容易　g. 我**们有**一点不喜欢这个工**作**

4. Character Jumble

a. 中国人　**b.**有意思　c. 工作室　d. 家庭主夫　e. 售货员　f. 大公司

5. Guided writing – write 3 short paragraphs describing the people below using the details in the box [in first person]

Luo Li: 我爸爸叫 Luo Li。他是老师。他爱他的工作，因为很有意思。

Luo Si: 我哥哥叫 Luo Si。他是工人。他不喜欢他的工作，因为没意思。

Kai Li: 我妈妈叫 Kai Li。她是护士。她喜欢她的工作，因为很重要。

6. Describe this person in Chinese in the 3rd person:

她叫 Mag。她有白色的头发。她很高，也很苗条。她很大方。她是医生。她非常喜欢她的工作，因为很有意思。

Grammar Time 6: Drills (Page 90)

Match up

很累 – **very tiring**　不重要 – **not important**　但是 – **but**　很忙 – **very busy**　有压力 – **stressful**
觉得 – **think/feel**

2. Rewrite the sentences into the correct order

a. 她喜欢这个工作，但是觉得很忙。　　b. 爸爸是医生，但是妈妈不是。

c. 姐姐有金发，可是我有黑头发。　　d. 猫很可爱，可是我喜欢狗。

e. 他们是中国人，但是住在英国。　　f. 他很友好，但是有一点无聊。

3. Translate into Chinese (easier)

a. 我哥哥很高，但是不帅。　　b. 我妈妈是护士…　c. 但是我爸爸是医生。

d. 我姐姐在公司工作。　　e. …但是我妹妹在医院工作。

f. 我的狗很可爱，但是我的猫很凶。

4. Spot and correct the grammar and character errors

a. 我们**是**朋友，**但**是我们的关系不好。　　b. **护**士的工作**很**忙，**可**是很有意思。

c. 我的工作**很**忙，**但是非常**重要　d. 他是我哥哥，可**是**我不喜**欢**他，**因**为他**很**帅。　　e. 我姐姐在一个学校工作，**但**是不是老**师**。

5. Translate into Chinese (harder)

a. 他是我爸爸的弟弟，但是我不喜欢他　b. 他是工程师，但是他姐姐是老师

c. 她有棕色的眼睛，但是她的弟弟有蓝色的眼睛　d. 我妈妈喜欢这个工作，但是觉得有一点难

e. 我爸爸喜欢这个工作，但是觉得非常忙　f. 爸爸有白头发，因为他的工作非常有压力

6. Translate into English

a. My friend likes this job, but thinks it's very tiring.

b. Being a doctor is a good job, but it's very busy and also very difficult.

c. My little brother is generous, but I think he is a bit annoying.

d. The US is good, and the UK also, but I like China the most.

e. He is an engineer, but he thinks it's not interesting to work in a company.

Unit 9 - Comparing people's appearance and personality

Revision Quickie 2: Family / Pets / Jobs

Unit 9. Comparing people: VOCABULARY BUILDING (Page 95)

1. Translate into English

a. My grandson   b. My boyfriend   c. My uncle   d. My daughter

e. My best friend   f. My friend   g. clever   h. young   i. happy

2. Complete with the missing word

a. 我爸爸比我哥哥**高**。   b. 我妈妈**没有**我阿姨幽默。   c. 我爷爷**比**我爸爸矮。

d. 他们**比**我们**忙**。   e. 我的猫**和**我的狗**一样**好玩。   f. 我阿姨**没有**我**妈妈**漂亮。

g. 我儿子**和**我**一样**强

3. Match Chinese and English

强 – strong   好看 – good-looking   友好 – kind   弱 – weak   老 – old   年轻 – young

幽默 – humorous

4. Spot and correct any English translation mistakes

a. ~~He is~~ **you are** taller than ~~you~~ **him**   b. ~~he is better looking than~~ **you are as good-looking as** ~~me~~ **her**

c. ~~he~~ **she** is ~~stronger than~~ **not as strong as** me

d. I am ~~fatter~~ **skinnier** than ~~him~~ **them**   e. ~~they~~ **you lot** are ~~happier than~~ **as happy as** us

f. She is as ~~old~~ **humorous** as ~~dad~~ **grandad**   g. ~~You are~~ **I am** not as clever as ~~them~~ **you**

5. Complete with a suitable word and translate into English

a. 我妈妈**很**高，也非常美。 - My mum is tall, and also extremely beautiful

b. 我爸爸**比**我叔叔年轻。 - My dad is younger than my uncle

c. 我孙女**和**我孙子**一样**好看。 - My grand-daughter is as good-looking as my grandson

d. 我弟弟**比**他聪明。 - My older brother is more clever than him

e. 我们的鸟**没有**我们的鱼安静。 - Our bird isn't as quiet as our fish

6. Match the opposites

好 - **坏**   好看 - **丑**   弱 - **强**   好玩 – **无聊**   年轻 – **老**   瘦 – **胖**   有意思 – 没意思

Unit 9. Comparing people: READING (Page 96)

1. Find the Chinese for the following in Jacky's text

a. 我住在   b. 我爸爸妈妈   c. 强   d. 帅   e. 非常亲切   f. 但是

g. 和妈妈一样好玩   h. 一只兔子   i. 两个宠物   j. 安静

2. Complete the statements below based on Chee Cheng's text

a. I am **20** years old   b. Mei is more **beautiful** than Leng

c. Mei is not as **kind** as Leng   d. My parents are very **friendly** and **fun**

e. I am as **humorous** as my father   f. We have **two** pets

3. Correct any of the statements below [about Joan's text] which are incorrect

a. Joan 有**两只**宠物。   b. James 比 Henry **瘦**。   c. Henry 比 James **幽默**。

d. James 和我家的狗一样**忙**。   e. Joan 的妈妈比爸爸**大方**。

4. Answer the questions on the three texts above

a. In a city   b. Mei   c. Jacky   d. Joan   e. Chee Cheng   f. Jacky

g. Chee Cheng   h. James   i. James is skinnier and shorter than Henry, but James is more humorous.

Unit 9. Comparing people: TRANSLATION/WRITING (Page 97)

1. Translate into English

a. tall   b. skinny   c. short   d. fat   e. girlfriend   f. young   g. grandson   h. daughter   i. the same

j. brothers   k. sisters

2. Gapped sentences

a. 我妈妈比我阿姨高。   b. 我爸爸比我哥哥强。   c. 我姐妹没有我友好。   d. 我的朋友比我高兴

e. 我妈妈和我爸爸一样亲切   f. 我的狗比我们忙

3. Phrase-level translation (English to Chinese)

a. 我妈妈是…   b. 比我高   c. 和你一样苗条   d. 没有她好玩   e. 我没有你高

f. 我爸爸妈妈是…   g. 我的兄弟是   h. 没有我们胖   i. 和他们一样高兴   j. 我爷爷奶奶是…

k. 我比他可爱

4. Sentence-level translation (English to Chinese)

a. 我姐姐比我妹妹高   b. 我孙子和他妈妈一样好看   c. 我女儿没有我烦人

d. 我没有我姐姐聪明   e. 我最好的朋友没有我忙   f. 我男朋友比我好看

g. 我的猫比他的猫丑   h. 我的狗比我的鸟胖   i. 我的猫比我的鱼好玩

j. 我的兔子比我的蛇老

Revision Quickie 2: Family, Pets and Jobs (Page 98)

1. Match

厨师 – chef   **家庭主妇** – housewife   **护士** – nurse   **工程师** – engineer   **售货员** – shop assistant

演员 – actor   **家庭主夫** – househusband   **医生** - doctor

2. Sort the words listed below in the categories in the table

Descriptions: b, d, i, j, k, l, p, r, s, v, w, x   **Animals:** o, t   **Work:** a, c, g, m, n

Family: e, f, h, q, u

3. Complete with the missing adjectives

a. 我爸爸很**胖**   b. 我妈妈很**高**   c. 我的狗很**烦人**   d. 我的老师很**老**

4. Complete with the missing nouns

a. 我叔叔是**商人**   b. 我奶奶是**护士**   c. 我的朋友是**画家**   d. 我姐姐是**医生**

e. 我弟弟是**司机**

5. Match the opposites

友好 – **凶**　胖 – **瘦**　孙子 – **孙女**　女儿 – **儿子**　高 – **矮**

年轻 – **老**　好玩 – **无聊**　好看 – **难看**

6. Spot and correct the mistakess

a. ~~一四~~ **十四**　b. ~~匹千~~ **四十**　c. ~~天十~~ **六十**　d. ~~五五~~ **五十五**

7. Complete with the correct verb or adverb

a. 我妈妈**很**高。　b. 我**有**黑头发。　c. 他们**是**工人。　d. 她的爸爸**是**中国人。

e. 你家**有**几个人？　f. 我的朋友**叫** Max Wong。　g. 我哥哥没**有**工作。

Unit 10 - Saying what's in my schoolbag

Grammar Time 7: Measure Words

Grammar Time 8: Saying "and" with 和

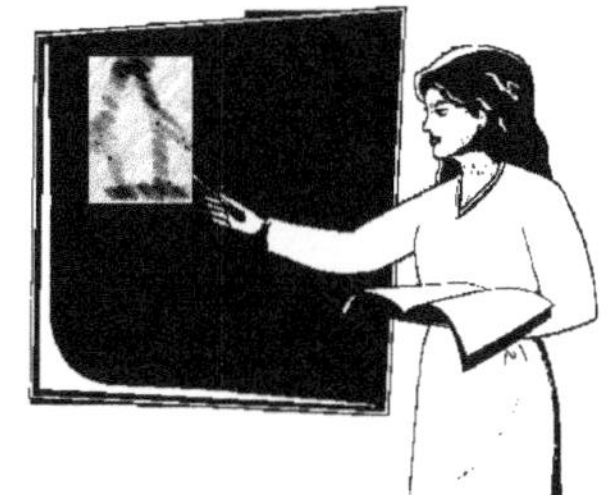

Unit 10. Saying what's in my schoolbag: VOCAB BUILDING (Page 103)

1. Complete with the missing word

a. 书包里有一本书。　b. 我要一把尺子。　c. 我没有笔。　d. 我的朋友有一把剪刀。

e. 我没有椅子。

2. Match up

学生 – **student**　椅子 – **chair**　一支笔 – **a pen**　两张桌子 – **two tables**　很多 – **lots of**

剪刀 – **scissors**　一些 – **some**

3. Translate into English

a. I have a Chinese writing brush　b. My teacher has lots of books　c. I don't have any rulers

d. I have two pens　e. I don't have any scissors　f. I want a table

g. There are students in the classroom　h. There are lots of books in the schoolbag

4. Add the missing tone marks

a. yì zhī máobǐ　b. wǒde péngyou　c. yì xiē xuésheng　d. yì bǎ jiǎndāo　e. hěn duō dōngxi

f. shūbāo lǐ　g. liǎng ge lǎoshī　h. méi yǒu bǐ

5. Add the missing components

a. 五支笔　b. 椅子　c. 毛笔　d. 两张桌子　e. 六把尺子　f. 一些学生

6. Broken Pinyin

a. shū bāo lǐ / yǒu / liǎng / běn / shū　b. shū bāo lǐ / yǒu / yì xiē / bǐ　c. hěn duō / yǐ zi

d. wǒ / méi yǒu / chí zi　e. xué sheng / yǒu / máo bǐ　f. wǒ / yǒu / yì xiē / shū

g. jiào shì lǐ / yǒu / hěn duō / dōngxi

7. Complete with a suitable word

a. 我有一本**书**。　b. 书包里有两**支**红笔。　c. 书包**里**有笔。　d. 教室里有一**张**桌子，也有一**把**椅子。　e. 学生有很**多**书。

Unit 10. Saying what's in my schoolbag: READING (Page 104)

1. Highlight the Chinese in Giulia's text

a. 我是　b. 我住在南非　c. 有四个人　d. 白色的猫　e. 红色的笔

f. 绿色的书　g. 我最喜欢　h. 一支笔　i. 一个好学生

2. Find Someone Who – which person…

a. Carmen　b. Alodie　c. Carmen　d. Alodie　e. Hugo　f. Carmen

3. Answer the following questions about Hugo's text

a. northern part of the US　b. his little brother　c. 20 tables and 20 chairs.　d. very beautiful

e. a whiteboard, tables and chairs　f. his teacher

4. Fill in the table below

Giulia: job – student   **country** – centre of South Africa   **items in classroom/bag** – a red pen, a green book and a ruler.

Alodie: job – teacher   **country** – France   **items in classroom/bag** –schoolbags, pens, Chinese writing brushes, 30 chairs and 30 tables

Unit 10. Saying what's in my schoolbag: TRANSLATION (Page 105)

1. Faulty translation: spot and correct [IN THE ENGLISH] any translation mistakes you find below

a. In my classroom there is a table and ~~a computer~~ **two pens**. I like my teacher.

b. I have many things in my schoolbag, there ~~is a~~ **are** two red ~~pencils~~ **pens**, but no ~~pens~~ **scissors**.

c. My friend has ~~five~~ **six** people in his family. He wants ~~a pen~~ **three books** and ~~a ruler~~ **Chinese writing brush**.

d. I need a ~~table~~ **chair** and a ~~chair~~ **ruler**. I don't have a ~~ruler~~ **schoolbag**. I ~~like~~ **dislike** my teacher!

e. In my class there are thirty **tables** ~~cats~~ and thirty chairs. I need a ~~calculator~~ **diary** but I **do** have a dictionary.

2. Translate into English

a. I want   b. I have a black pencil   c. I don't have a blue pen   d. A green ruler   e. I have a dog at home

f. My friend has a book   g. My dad is...   h. I really like my teacher   i. Some brown pencils

j. The classroom is (very) big   k. I have many things

3. Phrase-level translation (English to Chinese)

a. 五本书   b. 我有   c. 很多学生   d. 我的朋友没有   e. 老师喜欢   f. 一些笔

g. 书包里有…   h. 教室里有…

4. Sentence-level translation (English to Chinese)

a. 教室里有很多学生   b. 书包里有两支笔   c. 书包里有很多东西   d. 我有一些比

e. 我有一些毛笔   f. 我有两本书和一支笔   g. 我要一把椅子和一张桌子   h. 我爸爸是老师

i. 我的教室不大

Unit 10. Saying what's in my schoolbag: WRITING (Page 106)

1. Split sentences

我有一支**毛笔**   我的老师**非常亲切**   教室里没**有椅子**   **有三十二**张桌子   我的朋**友很可爱**

不是我**的书包**   我有一把**椅子**

2. Rewrite the sentences in the correct order

a. 我要三张桌子。   b. 我有五支笔和一把尺子。   c. 我的教室很大。

d. 我的朋友有一本书。   e. 我不要两把椅子。   F. 我家里有七条大蛇。

3. Spot and correct the grammar and characters [note: in several cases characters are missing]

a. 教室里有**两张**桌子。   b. 我有一个黑色的书**包**。   c. 我的朋**友**的书**包**里有笔。

d. 我的朋友**没有剪刀**。　　e. 我要一**支**笔和两本书。　　f. 我的老**师**有一**些**笔，也有很**多**尺子。

4. Pinyin Search

t	q	l	f	y	o	h	l
q	j	i	a	o	s	h	i
u	p	m	a	o	b	i	q
y	i	b	e	n	s	h	u
z	o	b	c	g	v	h	w
x	y	u	d	v	z	h	i

5. Guided writing – write 4 short paragraphs describing the people below using the details in the box [I]

Natalia: 我叫 Natalia。我住在法国。我有一本书。我没有笔。我要一把尺子。

Fei: 我叫 Fei。我住在中国。我有一把尺子。我没有书包。我要一支毛笔。

Juliet: 我叫 Juliet。我住在英国。我有一支红笔。我没有毛笔。我要一些黑笔。

6. Describe this person in Spanish:

他叫 Diego。他家有一只白狗。他有黑色的头发。他有两支红笔和一把尺子。他么有书包，也没有椅子。我最喜欢的颜色是红色。

Grammar Time 7: Measure Words: Drills (1) (Page 108)

1. Split sentences

三本**书**　　我要一**把椅子**　　两把**尺子**　　她要**五条蛇**　　他有十张**桌子**　　我要三**支毛笔**　　它是一**只狗**

四条**小鱼**

2. Complete with the missing word (pets and family members)

a. 我有三**只**宠物，两**条**鱼和一**只**狗。　　b. 一个中国人。　　c. 工厂里有二十个工人。

d. 你有几**个**兄弟姐妹？

3. Spot and correct the measure words (note: nota ll sentences are wrong)

a. 你有一**支**毛笔吗？　　b. 我要两**本**书。　　c. 书包里有两把尺子。　**CORRECT**

d. 教室里有三个老师。　**CORRECT**　　e. 我们有六**条**鱼，一只小猫和两只狗。

f. 我有三个阿姨。　**CORRECT**　　g. 他们有四把剪刀、四**张**桌子。

h. 我姐姐有两个书包。　**CORRECT**

4. Write the correct MW in the gap

a. 条　b. 只　c. 本　d. 把　e. 支　f. 个　g. 张

5. Translate into Chinese

a. 我爸爸有两个弟弟　　b. 我有四只宠物　　c. 他们有六支笔　　d. 我书包里有一把尺子

e. 你有尺子吗？　　f. 我家有一只狗和一只鸟　　g. 教室里有四个老师　　h. 学生有五本书

i. 他有三把椅子和两张桌子　j.我要十支毛笔

Measure Words and use of 有 and 是: Drills (2) (Page 109)

6. Translate the pronoun <u>and</u> verb into Chinese as shown in the example

I have: **我有**　you don't have: **你们没有**　she has: **她有**　he has: **他有**

we have: **我们有**　You guys have: **你们有**　Those guys have: **他们有**

Those girls don't have: **她们没有**

7. Translate into Chinese. Topic: Pets and colours

a. 我们有三只红鸟　b. 我有两条绿蛇　c. 我哥哥有一只白色的大狗　d. 我姐姐有两只黑猫

e. 我妹妹有一只红黑鸟　f. 我们家有六只宠物　g. 你家有几只宠物？

8. Translate into Chinese. Topic: family members

a. 我有三个哥哥　b. 我们有两个爷爷　c. 我妈妈有一个妹妹　d. 你有几个兄弟姐妹？

e. 你们有几个弟弟？　F. 我有五个好朋友

9. Complete with the missing words

a. 他是一个中国人。　b. 他们有两只狗。　c. 我爸爸有六只鸟　d. 你妈妈有几条鱼？

e. 我没有两只宠物。　f. 我有一只宠物。　g. 我有很多朋友。　h. 你有几只宠物？

10. Spot and correct the grammar errors

a. 我妈妈**五十岁**，她是**中国人**。　b. 我有**一些**白头发。　c. 教室里有**一把**椅子和一张桌子。

d. 我的书包里有**一支**笔和一本书。　e. 我**十三岁**，我有两**个**好朋友。

Grammar Time 8: Saying "and" with 和 (Page 110)

1. Translate into English

a. dad and me　b. I like dogs and fish　c. My and him have schoolbags

d. Chinese people and American people　e. My grandfather and grandmother are both 88 years old

f. May and August　g. I have a dog and three cats

2. Translate into Chinese

a. 一支红笔和一本书　b. 一把黑尺子和两支毛笔　c. 一个书包和两本书

d. 十二把椅子和十一只狗　e. 两把尺子和一个姐姐　f. 两本蓝书和十五条鱼

g. 两本红书和两个书包　h. 两只白猫和一条黑蛇　i. 一个书包和一些东西

6. Spot and correct the grammar errors

a. 我爸爸五十岁。**他**是中国人。　b. 我们**有**一只白猫和两只大狗。

c. 我的生日是五月六日。**我十五岁**。　d. 书包里有一把尺子、两本书**和**三支笔。

e. 我们有两**个**好朋友，一个是英格兰人，一个是苏格兰人。

f. 我们是英国人。我们住在英国**的**北部。　g.我是一个很友好的人，**可是**他不是。

Unit 11 - Talking about food (Part 1): Likes/ Dislikes / Reasons

Grammar Time 9: "or" 或者 vs. 还是

Unit 11. Talking about food (Part 1): VOCABULARY BUILDING (Part 1) (Page 115)

1. Match up

面条 – **noodles**　米饭 – **rice**　肉 – **meat**　水 – **water**　汽水 – **fizzy drinks**　果汁 – **fruit juice**

牛奶 – **milk**　水果 – **fruit**　咖啡 – **coffee**　奶茶 – **milk tea**　中国茶 – **Chinese tea**

2. Complete with the missing characters

a. 我喜欢**吃**面包　b. 我**爱**吃点**心**　c. 我喜**欢**吃米饭　d. 我爱喝**牛奶**　e. 我爱**吃面**条

f. 我**更**喜欢喝**水**

3. Translate into English

a. I don't like fruit that much　b. Fizzy drinks are not healthy

c. I like to drink milk because it is very healthy　d. My grandmother loves eating dim sum

e. My dad most likes to drink coffee　f. I like noodles a bit

g. We don't like to drink fruit juice because it's not nice to drink

4. Rewrite the characters so they include the missing parts

a.**汽水**　b.**面条**　c.**咖啡**　d.**喝**　e.**吃**

5. Choose either 吃 or 喝 as appropriate to complete the sentence

a.**吃**　b.**喝**　c.**喝**　d.**喝, 喝**　e.**吃**　f.**吃**

6. Translate into Chinese

a. 我爱吃米饭　b. 我更爱吃水果　c. 我不喜欢吃肉　d. 我不喜欢喝果汁　e. 我最喜欢吃面条

f. 不好吃　g. 不好喝

Unit 11. Talking about food (Part 1): VOCABULARY BUILDING (Part 2) (Page 116)

1. Complete with the missing character

a. 这个面**包**很难**吃**　b. 苹果非常健康　c. 我不喜欢吃**肉**　d. 这个咖啡很**好**喝

e.**青**菜很健康，也很好吃　f. 我**不**喜欢喝**汤**　g. 我**爱**喝牛奶

2. Complete the table

果汁 – **fruit juice**　肉 – meat　难吃 – **not nice to eat**　茶 – **tea**　水 – water　面条 – noodles

喝汤 – **have soup (accept 'drink soup')**　吃点心 – **eat dim sum**　米饭 – rice

3. Change the Pinyin into Chinese character to complete the Word

a.**牛奶**　b.**面条**　c.**青菜**　d.**米饭**　e.**汽水**　f.**喜欢**　g.**咖啡**　h.**果汁**　i.**水果**

4. Broken pinyin

a. wǒ / bù / xǐhuan / chī / yú   b. wǒ / ài / hē / kā fēi   c. yīn wèi / tāng / bù / hǎo hē

d. wǒ / gèng / xǐ huan / mǐ fàn   e. diǎn xīn / hěn / hǎo chī   f. yú / hěn / jiàn kāng

g. wǒ / bù / hē / qì shuǐ

Unit 11. Talking about food (Part 1): READING (Page 117)

1. Find the Chinese for the following in Roberta's text

a. 我爱吃鱼   b. 我更爱喝鱼汤   c. 我也喜欢   d. 牛肉汤   e. 都很好喝   f. 我有一点喜欢   g. 也爱

h. 最喜欢   i. 因为很难吃

2. Monica or Roberta? Write M or R next to each statement below

a. *Roberta*   b. Monica   c. Monica   d. Roberta   e. Roberta   f. Monica   g. Monica   h. Monica

3. Complete the following sentences based on Raine's text

a. Rain loves **vegetables**   b. She thinks they are **tasty and also healthy**

c. She also likes **fruit** because it is **tasty**   d. She dislikes **meat** and **fish**

e. She thinks they are healthy but **not tasty/not nice to eat**

4. Fill in the table below about Xin Yan and Mia

Xin Yan: Loves – meat   **Likes a lot** – beef, dim sum   **Doesn't like** – tea

Mia: Loves – meat, bread   **Likes a lot** – burgers, spaghetti (Italian noodles/pasta), pizza   **Doesn't like** – vegetables, fizzy drinks

Unit 11. Talking about food (Part 1): TRANSLATION (Page 118)

1. Faulty translation: spot and correct [IN THE ENGLISH] any translation mistakes you find below

a. I ~~hate~~ **dislike** fish **a little**   b. ~~I~~ **We** like **eating** meat   c. I ~~don't~~ **most** like to drink water

d. I **don't** love ~~apples~~ **fruit**   e. ~~Fruit~~ **Fruit juice** is tastier   f. ~~banana~~ **Fruit juice** is **extremely** healthy

g. **Because** ~~fish~~ **fizzy drinks** are unhealthy   h. I prefer ~~water~~ **tea**

i. I love **fruit and** vegetables   j. I love ~~rice~~ **noodles**   k. I **don't** ~~quite~~ like soup **that much**

2. Translate into English

a. Fish is extremely tasty   b. Dim sum is most delicious   c. Because meat is very healthy

d. Chinese people love rice   e. Meat is extremely unhealthy   f. I want to eat some bread

g. Fizzy drinks are not nice to drink   h. I prefer water   i. I like drinking milk a bit

j. I don't like vegetables that much   k. I most like Chinese tea   l. This soup is very tasty

3. Phrase-level translation (English to Chinese)

a. 吃面条   b. 茶，不是咖啡   c. 我很喜欢   d. 很好吃   e. 一个不好吃的苹果   f. 一些好吃的点心

g. 我不太喜欢吃鱼   h. 我爱   i. 面包和水   j. 喝汤   k. 肉和青菜

4. Sentence-level translation (English to Cbinese)

a. 我很喜欢吃面条   b. 我喜欢水果，因为很好吃   c. 我觉得肉很好吃，但是姐姐不太喜欢

d. 我喜欢吃面条，因为很好吃   e. 鱼很难吃   f. 我爱吃水果，因为水果很好吃

g. 我爱吃鱼，因为鱼很好吃   h. 我不太爱吃青菜   i. 我更喜欢吃肉   j. 红茶不好喝

Unit 11. Talking about food (Part 1): WRITING (Page 119)

1. Split sentences

我爱喝**牛奶**   我不喜欢吃青**菜和鱼**   我更喜欢吃**面条**   因为水果**非常好吃**   我有一点喜**欢吃肉**

这一些点心很好**吃，但是不健康**   我爱吃米**饭和面条**

2. Rewrite the sentences in the correct order

a. 我爱喝牛奶。　　b. 我不太喜欢吃青菜。　　c. 水果很好吃。　　d. 水很好喝，但是茶更好喝。

e. 我更喜欢吃点心。

3. Pinyin search

m	i	a	n	t	i	a	o
i	i	i	a	o	s	h	i
a	p	f	a	o	a	i	q
n	i	b	a	n	h	h	u
b	o	n	a	n	c	h	i
a	y	u	d	v	a	h	I
o	s	h	u	i	g	u	o

4. Spot and correct the grammar and character mistakes

a. 我没**不爱**吃米饭 b. 我~~门~~们~~受~~**爱**喝~~气~~**汽水**   c. 我不吃鱼，因很~~没~~**不好吃** d. 我~~便~~**更**喜欢喝茶 e. 我有一~~古~~**点**喜吃茶和吃~~古~~**点**心

5. Guided writing – write 4 short paragraphs describing the pets below using details in the box [I]

Doreen: 我叫 Doreen。我爱吃鱼，因为鱼很好吃。我有一点喜欢吃面条，更喜欢吃水果。我不喜欢吃肉，因为肉不好吃。

Wen Di: 我叫 Wen Di。我爱喝水，因为好喝。我有一点喜欢喝汤，但是更喜欢喝果汁。我不喜欢吃米饭，因为米饭很难吃。

Eric: 我叫 Eric，我最喜欢吃米饭因为很好吃。我有一点喜欢吃面条，但是我更喜欢吃点心。我很不喜欢吃青菜，因为不好吃。

6. Write a paragraph on Qiu Mei in Chinese [using the third person singular]

她叫 Qiu Mei，她十八岁。她很高，也很友好。她是一个学生。她爱吃米饭，也喜欢吃青菜。她不喜欢吃肉。她非常不喜欢/讨厌吃鱼。

Grammar Time 9: Drills (Page 121)

1. Match

红茶 – red tea   **苹果** – apple   **或者** – or (statement)   **水果** – fruit   **还是** – or (question)

果汁 – fruit juice   **绿茶** – green tea

2. Translate into English

a. likes noodles   b. drinks apple juice or tea   c. I don't drink coffee   d. eats a lot of fish
e. We drink water   f. They don't eat meat   g. I eat rice everyday   h. Would you like meat or
vegetables? i. Do you want to eat or to drink?   j. I would like to drink fruit juice or milk

3. Spot and correct the mistakes

a. 你爸爸吃面条或者~~还是~~面包？   b. 他和我不吃青菜，也**不吃**水果。   c. 妈妈想吃**喝**汤还是喝
茶？   d. 喝**吃**苹果还是吃**喝**苹果汁比较健康呢？   e. 我不要喝啡咖或者茶。

f. 他的生日是一月还是二月？

4. 或者 or 还是?

a. 还是   b. 还是   c. 或者   d. 或者   e. 还是   f. 还是

5. Translate into Chinese [easier]

a. 我喜欢吃米饭或者面条   b. 我们更喜欢喝水或者果汁   c. 你们更喜欢吃肉还是青菜？

d. 茶还是咖啡？   e. 她不喜欢吃水果或者喝果汁   f. 他们不吃很多肉或者

6. Translate into Chinese [harder]

a. 我不吃肉或者米饭，因为我不喜欢   b. 我不喝咖啡肉或者汽水，因为不好喝

c. 我喝水或者果汁，因为很健康   d. 星期五或者星期六我们吃鱼。我爱吃鱼，因为很好吃

e. 青菜还是水果？我爸爸都喜欢，但是我不喜欢

f. 米饭还是面包？两个都好吃，但是我更喜欢吃面条   g. 星期五我爱吃鱼，因为鱼非常好吃

Unit 12 - Talking about food (Part 2): Likes / Dislikes / Reasons

Grammar Time 10: Saying "everyday" with 每天都

Grammar Time 11: Saying "both" and "all" with 都

Question Skills 2: Jobs / Schoolbag / Food

Unit 12. Talking about food – Likes/Dislikes (Part 2): VOCABULARY (Page 126)

1. Match

蛋糕 - cake   水果 - fruit   牛肉 - beef   饺子 - dumplings   羊肉 - lamb   烤鸭 - roast duck

猪肉 - pork   沙拉 - salad   海鲜 - seafood   鸡蛋 - egg   蔬菜 - vegetables

2. Complete with the missing words

a. 肉**比**海鲜好吃   b. 我最爱吃**蔬菜**   c. 我更喜欢吃猪**肉**   d. 我**早**饭吃**米**饭   e. 鸡**肉**很好吃

f. 烤**鸭**特别好吃

3. Change the pinyin into characters to complete the words

a. 汽**水** b. **牛**肉 c. **水**果 d. **午**饭 e. 苹**果** f. 鸡**肉** g. **牛**奶 h. **米**饭 i. **晚**饭 j. 饺**子**

4. Match up

面条 - **noodles**   早饭 - **breakfast**   烤 - roast   难吃 - **not tasty**   好吃 - **delicious**   健康 - **healthy**

饺子 - **dumplings**   鸡汤 - **chicken soup**   蔬菜 - **vegetables**

5. Sort the items below in the appropriate category

Meat: d, h, p   **Meals:** f, l, n   **Adjectives:** a, c, m   **Four-based food:** i, o, q   **Drinks:** b, e, g, j, k, r

Unit 12. Talking about food – Likes/Dislikes (Part 2): READING (Part 1) (Page 127)

1. Find and highlight the Chinese for words listed below in Fen's text

a. egg - 鸡蛋   b. tea - 茶   c. coffee - 咖啡   d. friend - 朋友   e. lunch - 午饭   f. chicken - 鸡肉

g. bread – 面包   h. this – 这   i. but - 但是   j. Sunday - 星期天   k. vegetables - 蔬菜

l. healthy - 健康   m. cake - 蛋糕   n. dinner - 晚饭   o. rice - 米饭   p. think – 觉得

2. Complete the following sentences based on Fen's text

a. At breakfast I eat **egg** and **bread**.   b. Coffee is not as **healthy** as tea.   c. For lunch I eat **chicken** with **vegetables** and drink **water**.   d. I eat a lot of vegetables because they are **healthy** and delicious.

e. At dinner I love to eat **rice**, seafood or **fish** and **vegetables**. I also eat **cake**

f. This Sunday I am going to eat **roast chicken** because people say it **has** a lot of protein, but so does **vegetables**.   g. I think vegetables are much **healthier** than meat.

3. Find the Chinese for the following in Roberta/Fen's text

a. 我早饭吃很少   b. 我午饭吃   c. 鸡肉和蔬菜   d. 苹果汁   e. 沙拉   f. 牛肉比羊肉好吃

g. 一杯咖啡   h. 我是厨师   i. 米饭、海鲜或者鱼   j. 蛋糕   k. 饺子   l. 苹果或者面包

Unit 12. Talking about food – Likes/Dislikes (Part 2): READING (Part 2) (Page 128)

4. Who says this, Roberta or Fen? Or both?

a. Roberta   b. Roberta   c. Roberta   d. Roberta   e. Fen   f. Roberta, Fen   g. Fen   h. Fen   i. Fen
j. Roberta, Fen   k. Roberta   l. Fen

5. Answer the following questions on Wei Ling's text

a. a lot   b. an apple, 2 or 3 eggs, a toast   c. black   d. apple juice   e. chicken or fruit salad
f. because it is full of vitamins and healthy   g. dim sum, 2 slices of toasts, a cup of tea   h. because it's
not healthy

6. Find in Wei Ling's text the following:

a. 咖啡   b. 苹果   c. 水   d. 鸡肉   e. 沙拉   f. 茶   g. 好吃   h. 蛋糕   i. 早饭   j. 巧克力   k. 健康
l. 点心

Unit 12. Talking about food – Likes/Dislikes (Part 2): WRITING (Page 129)

1. Split sentences

我不吃羊肉   我早饭吃面条   我爱吃烤鸭和米饭   我喜欢吃沙拉   鱼比牛肉健康   饺子非常好吃
苹果是水果不是青菜   我喝茶不喝咖啡   多喝汽水

2. Complete with the correct option

a. 我晚饭爱吃海鲜，特别是虾   b. 我要吃青菜和牛肉面。   c. 我和家人星期天吃烤鸡肉。
d. 我午饭吃鱼和鸡肉。   e. 我早饭吃鸡蛋，喝牛奶。

3. Spot and correct the grammar and character mistakes [note: in several cases characters are missing]

a. 我早反饭吃两个面包，也喝苹果十汁。   b. 我喝果汁或者喝吃苹果。
c. 牛内肉非常好吃非常，可是不建健康。
d. 我爱吃水果沙拉，因为是很好吃。   e. 放学后，我常常吃烤面包常常。
f. 我喝茶，也喝牛仍奶，你呢？   g. 我爱吃交饺子和考烤鸭。
h. 我晚饭吃喝汤、吃鱼和蔬彩菜。

4. Rewrite the characters so they include their missing parts

a. 午饭   b. 晚饭   c. 海鲜   d. 蔬菜

5. Guided writing – write 3 short paragraphs in the first person [I] using the details below

Ade: 我叫 Ade。我午饭吃鸡肉和米饭。我也喝牛奶，因为非常好喝

Jaha: 我叫 Jaha。我午饭喜欢吃猪肉和面条，因为我觉得很好吃。 我也喝汽水。

Issa: 我叫 Issa。我午饭喜欢吃青菜、喝汤。 我也喝水因为喝水比较健康。

6. Sentence level translation (English – Chinese)

a. 我吃面条。   b. 我早饭吃面包。   c. 我喜欢吃鱼，也爱吃鸡肉。

Challenge: d. 我吃牛肉，但是不吃鸡肉。   e. 我喝黑咖啡，因为很健康。

Grammar Time 10: Driills (Page 130-131)

1. Choose the correct word in each sentence

a. 他们每**天**都喝咖啡。　　b. 我每天**都**吃早饭，因为**很**健康。

c. 我们**每**天都喝奶茶，因为**很**好喝。　　d. 他们**每天**都吃**苹果**，也喝果汁。

e. 你们**每天**都吃米饭吗？

2. Insert the given word into the appropriate place of each sentence

a. 奶奶每天**都**喝茶。　　b. 爸爸和爷爷**每**天都喝桔子汁。　　c. 他每天**都**喝水和茶。

d. 他们**每天**都吃牛肉和米饭。　　e. 你们每天**都**吃什么？　　f. 我和他**每天**都吃水果。

3. Spot and correct the errors with the verbs 喝 and 吃

a. 我喜欢吃**喝**一杯咖啡。　　b. 他每天都喝汤和喝**吃**点心。　　c. 我们每天都喝**吃**饺子。

d. 她每天都喝**吃**水果。　　e. 妈妈要我们每天都吃**喝**水。　　f. 我爸爸每天都**吃**牛肉和面条。

g. 我男朋友每天都**吃**肉。

4. Translate into English

a. My mother eats fruit everyday.　b. They eat a lot everyday.

c. You drink lots of coffee everyday, (which is) very unhealthy.

d. We eat five oranges and drink milk tea everyday.

e. My younger brother drinks iced tea everyday, but he doesn't drink wáter.

f. My son eats takeaways everyday but he doesn't eat vegetables.

g. My mother drinks hot water everyday because hot water is healthier than fizzy drinks.

i. Auntie is fat because she eats junk food everyday.　j. I eat apples everyday.

5. Translate into Chinese

a.我每天都吃　b. 我们每天都吃　c. 他们每天都　d. 她每天都吃早饭　e. 我们每天都吃晚饭

f. 你午饭吃…　g. 每个月他们吃　h. 每个水果都好吃

6. Translate into Chinese

a. 我每天早饭都吃面包和水果。　　b. 我朋友每天都吃鸡肉和米饭。

c. 我们每天都吃很多。我们喜欢吃鱼和面条。

Challenge:

a. 他们每天都吃外卖。　　B. 我每天吃沙拉，因为我不吃肉。

c. 我爸爸吃很多肉，但是我妈妈和我每天都吃青菜。　　d. 他们每天喝汤，不吃海鲜或者面包。

e. 弟弟觉得吃垃圾食品很健康！

Grammar Time 11: Drills (Page 133)

1. Make the sentences below grammatically correct by including 都

a. 鱼和海鲜都非常好吃。　　b. 他们都不吃外卖。　　c. 我们都是美国人。

d. 牛肉和猪肉饺子都好吃。　　e. 我女儿和儿子都喜欢小狗。

f. 她们两个都爱穿高跟鞋。

41

2. Tick off the correct sentences and correct the incorrect ones

a.✓鱼和肉都非常好吃。　b. 我们**都**吃都面条和米饭。　c.✓书和笔都在书包里。

d. 都水果沙拉和青菜**都**很好吃。　e.✓姐姐和哥哥**都**是老师。　f. 我要鸡蛋和蛋糕**我都要**。

3. Rewrite the sentences in the correct order

a. 我们都喜欢喝果汁和水。　b. 妈妈和爸爸都不喜欢喝茶。　c. 他们都是中国人。

d. 我们都不喜欢吃面条。　e. 这些东西都很好吃。

4. Translate into English

a. She and I are both British.　b. They all want to eat oranges.　c. We all have books and pens.

d. Both father and younger brother like beef noodles.　e. Rice and noodles are both good to eat.

5. Translate into Chinese

a. 鱼和面条都不好吃　b. 他们都喜欢吃水果　c. 咖啡和茶都很好喝　d. 点心和蛋糕都很好吃

e. 我们都喜欢果汁　f. 爸爸和我都不喜欢他们　g. 妈妈和我都爱吃蛋糕

Question Skills 2: Jobs/Schoolbag/Food (Page 137)

1. Translate into English

a. What job does your dad do?　b. What do you like to eat?　c. What does he want to drink?

d. What does he want to eat?　e. Where does she work?　f. Why don't you like coffee?

g. What's in his schoolbag?　h. How many teachers does he have?

i. How many students are in the Chinese classroom?　j. How many books are in the schoolbag?

k. Do you want to drink water or tea?　l. Where does your uncle work?

m. Why does she like this book?　n. How many desks are in the classroom?

o. Where is your schoolbag?　p. What is your girlfriend like as a person?

q. Do you want to be a doctor or artist?　r. Where does she drink coffee?

s. Why don't you have a schoolbag?　t. What is your teacher like?

2. Match the answers below to the questions in activity 1

1. 书包里有三本书。**j** 2. 我想做医生。**q** 3. 因为咖啡不好喝，我比较喜欢喝茶。**f**

4. 我的女朋非常聪明，也很友好。**p** 5. 她在教室里喝咖啡。**r**

6. 我喜欢吃水果、饺子和牛肉。**b** 7. 我爸爸是护士。**a** 8. 我叔叔在学校工作。**l**

9. 我要喝茶，谢谢。**k** 　　10. 他想要喝果汁，谢谢。**c** 11. 我的老师非常友好，也很好玩。**t**

3. Provide the questions to the following answers

a. 你在哪儿工作？　b. 你喜欢吃青菜还是肉？ c. 教室里有几把椅子？　d. 他哥哥人怎么样？

e. 你妈妈做什么工作？　f. 你为什么不喝汽水？　g. 你为什么喜欢水果沙拉？

h. 书包里有几支笔？　i. 你要吃什么？　j 你哥哥在哪儿？

4. Tick off the correct questions and correct the incorrect ones

a. 你爸爸人什么**怎么样**？　b. 书包里有哪儿**几**本书？　c. 你想要吃什么？✓

d. 你**为**什么喜欢喝果汁？　e. 你要喝什么？✓ f. 他在哪儿工作？✓

g. 你喜欢红色的书包还是黑色的书包？✓　h. 你的男朋友人为什么**怎么样**？

Unit 13 - Talking about clothes and accessories I wear, how frequently and when

Grammar Time 12: Saying "when" with 的时候

Revision Quickie 3: Jobs, food, clothes, numbers 20-100

Unit 13. Talking about clothes: VOCABULARY BUILDING (Page 142)

1. Match up

鞋子 – **shoes**　毛衣 – **jumper**　手表 - **watch**　衬衣 - **shirt**　夹克 - **jacket**　裙子 - **skirt**

裤子 – **Trousers**

2. Complete with the missing word

a. 我穿衬**衣**。　 b. 在学校的时候，我穿黑色**的**裤**子**。　 c. 天气冷的时候，我穿**毛衣**。

d. 我很少穿**高**跟鞋。　 e. 我每天都打红色**的**领带。　 f. 我喜欢**戴**手表。

g. 我想**要**粉红色的袜子。　 h. 我**穿**裙子，也戴帽**子**。

3. Translate into English

a. I wear black socks　 b. I don't wear high heel shoes　 c. I wear a red hat　 d. I don't wear a watch

e. I rarely wear skirts　 f. I always wear jumpers　 g. I wear purple shoes and yellow socks

h. I wear a white shirt and pink trousers　 i.　We wear blue jackets and also wear belts

j. My mother often wears a pink hat　 k. Tomorrow my dad is going to wear an orange shirt

4. Associations – match each body part below with the words in the box, as shown in the examples.

a. 头*[head]* – **6. 帽子**　 b. 脚*[feet]* – **1. 袜子，7. 鞋子**　 c. 腿*[legs]* – **3.裤子**　 d. 手腕*[wrist]* – **2. 手表**

e. 脖子*[neck]* – **5. 领带**　 The one word without an association is **夹克**

5. Change the pinyin into a Chinese character to complete the phrase or sentence

a. 我穿白色的衬 **yī 衣**。　 b. **zài 在** ＿＿＿ 家的时候,… 。　 c. 我有 **shǒu 手**表

d. 我系黄色的皮 **dài 带**。

Unit 13. Talking about clothes: READING (Page 143)

1. Highlight the Chinese for the following in Lu Hui's text

a. 我住在　 b. 南部　 c. 因为　 d. 很多 T 恤　 e. 喜欢穿　 f. 在家的时候　 g. 和男朋友　 h. 红色的鞋子

i. 或者蓝色的毛衣

2. Highlight the Chinese for the following in Nathan's text

a. 和朋友出去玩的时候　 b. 我穿衬衣　 c. 蓝色的裤子和灰色的鞋子　 d. 在家　 e. 打领带

f. 天气热的时候　 g. 总是戴帽子　 h. 灰色的裤子　 i. 黑鞋子　 j. 常常

3. Complete the following statements about Zhao Fan

a. She is **thirteen** years old　 b. She is Chinese but **lives in the eastern part of the US**

c. When it's cold she wears a **black** or **purple coat** and **trousers**

d. She likes to wear white or **pink** shirt and **high heel shoes**   e. She often wears a **watch**

4. Answer in Chinese the questions below about Jiami

a. 她叫 Jiami。   b. 她是商人。   c. 她住在英国的北部。   d. 她喜欢穿裙子。   e. 她每天穿 T 恤

f. 天气冷的时候，她穿毛衣 g. 因为天气热。

5. Find someone who

a. Jiami b. Nathan c. Lu Hui d. Lu Hui e. Jiami f. Lu Hui g. Zhao Fan h. Jiami i. Jiami

Unit 13. Talking about clothes: WRITING (Page 144)

1. Split sentences

在**家的时候** 我系紫**色的皮带** 和朋友出**去玩的时候** 我们穿**橙色的裤子** 我不打**领带**

我爸爸常**常戴手表** 天气好**的时候** 我穿黄**色的毛衣**

2. Complete with the correct option

a. 和妈妈出去的时候，我穿裙**子**。   b. 在学校的时候，我**穿**白色的衬衫。

c. 在家**的**时候，我不穿鞋子。   d. 天气冷的时候，我穿**毛**衣。   e. 天气热的时候，我戴**帽**子。

3. Spot and correct the grammar and character mistakes [note: in several cases characters are missing]

a. 在家的时候，我穿袜**子** b. 我有很多鞋子**子** c. 和爸爸妈妈出去玩的时候，我戴紫色的冒**帽**子

d. 弟弟**不喜欢**打领带不喜欢 e. 在学校的候，我门**们**穿红色的猫**毛**衣

f. 和友朋**友**山**出**去玩的时候，我常常穿 T 血**恤** g. 天令**冷**的时候，我穿大**衣**和毛衣

4. Rewrite the characters so they include their missing parts

a. 裙子 [skirt]   b. 袜子 [socks]   c. 裤子 [trousers]   d. 灰色 [grey]

5. Guided writing – write 3 short paragraphs in the first person [I] using the details below

Yi Chen: 我叫 Yi Chen。我住在上海。我每天都穿黑色的毛衣，也穿裤子。我不喜欢打领带。

Ji Hua: 我叫 Ji Hua。我住在北京。我每天都穿白色的 T 恤和高跟鞋。我不喜欢戴手表。

Bao: 我叫 Bao。我住在西安。我每天都穿裙子，也穿毛衣。我不喜欢戴帽子。

6. Describe this person in Chinese using the 3rd person

他叫 Nate。他住在英国，他二十岁。他有一只黑色和白色的猫。他有棕色的头发。他总是穿衬衣，很少穿袜子或者毛衣。在学校的时候，他穿红色的夹克，也带手表。

Grammar Time 12: Drills (Page 145)

1. Spot and correct the errors

a. 左**在**家的时候 b. 公司的寸**时**候 c. **在学校**的时候在字校 d. 天令冷的时候

e. 夫**天**气热的时猴**候** f. 和朋**友**出去玩的**时**候 g. 在学交**校**的时候 h. 在叔叔家**的**时候

2. Rewrite the sentences in the correct order

a. 在家的时候，妈妈穿衬衣。   b. 和朋友出去玩的时候，我穿裙子。

c. 天气热的时候，学生穿白色的 T 恤。　d. 在公司的时候，爸爸穿夹克。

e. 天气热的时候，妹妹穿红色的裙子。　f. 天气冷的时候，老师穿黄色的毛衣。

g. 在学校的时候，老师打蓝色的领带。　h. 在公司的时候，爸爸穿白色的衬衣。

3. Mosaic Translation. Obtain the Chinese translation of the English sentences by selecting the appropriate tiles in the translation grid, as shown in the example

和朋友出去玩[e]	的时候，[e]	我们穿[e]	红色的[e]	大 T 恤[a]
和爸爸妈妈出去[d]	的时候，[d]	我穿[d]	常常穿[a]	戴帽子[b]
在学校[c]	的时候，[c]	我[a]	很少[b]	也系皮带[c]
天气冷[b]	的时候[a]	我爸爸[b]	戴手表[c]	裙子[d]
在家[a]	的时候，[b]	我哥哥[c]	黄色的[d]	袜子[e]

a.在家的时候，我常常穿大 T 恤　b.天气冷的时候，我爸爸很少戴帽子

c. 在学校的时候，我哥哥戴手表，也系皮带　d. 和爸爸妈妈出去的时候，我穿黄色的裙子

e. 和朋友出去玩的时候，我们穿红色的袜子

4. Translate into English

a. When at home　b. When at a friend's house　c. When the weather is good　d. When it is raining

e. When it is sunny

Challenge

a. When in China　b. When in the supermarket　c. When in the city

d. When watching TV with grandma

5. Translate into Chinese

a. 天气热的时候　b. 天气冷的时候　c. 在家的时候　d. 在公司的时候

Challenge

d. 我妈妈很少穿白色的裤子。　b. 我总是穿黄色的毛衣。　c.他常常系棕色的皮带。

d. 他们每天都穿绿色的夹克。　e. 在海边的时候，我不穿鞋子。

f. 天气冷的时候，我常常穿黄色的袜子。　g. 天气不好的时候，我们穿红色的鞋子。

Revision Quickie 3: Jobs, food, clothes and numbers 20-100 (Page 147)

1. Complete (numbers)

a. 100 – 一百　b. 90 – 九十　c. 30 – 三十　d. 50 – 五十　e. 80 – 八十

2. Translate into English (food and clothes)

a. coat   b. drink   c. chicken   d. skirt   e. vegetables   f. beef   g. seafood   h. fish   i. tie   j. shoes
k. fruit juice   l. dinner

3. Write in a word each letter in the categories below as shown in the example

s: 手表、蔬菜、四、司机

l: -、-、六、老师

q: 裙子、汽水

y: 衣服、羊肉/鸭肉、一、医生

w: 袜子、-、五、-

4. Match

我喝 - **I drink**   我叫 - **I am called**   我住在 - **I live**   我有 - **I have**   我是 - **I am**   我穿 - **I wear**

我吃 - **I eat**   我不是 - **I am not**   我没有 - **I don't have**   我戴 - **I wear (accessory)**

5. Translate into English

a. I am a nurse   b. I often eat dim sum   c. I rarely wear a skirt   d. I always drink coffee

e. I don't drink fizzy drinks   f. I eat eggs every day   g. My mother is a business person

h. I don't have green socks

Unit 14 - Saying what I and others do in our free time

Grammar Time 13: Using 每 and 都 to express frequency

Unit 14. Free time: VOCABULARY BUILDING – Part 1 (Page 152)

1. Match up

我每天都看书 - **I read everyday**　我看小说 – **I read a novel**

我打羽毛球 - **I play badminton**　我看报纸 - **I read the newspaper**

我玩滑板 - **I skateboard**　天气好 - **The weather is good**　我看电影 - **I watch movies**

我打篮球 - **I play basketball**

2. Complete with the missing word

a. 我**打**篮球　b. 天**气**好的时候　c. 我很**少**　d. 我**每**个星期　e. 我**有**时候　f. 我**和**妈妈**一**起

3. Translate into English

a. I skateboard everyday　b. Tomorrow my older sister and I are watching a movie together

c. We watch movies three times a month　d. My grandma rarely drinks coffee

e. When the weather is good, Dad and I play basketball together

f. My younger brother and I play ball games together every week

g. Grandfather and I sometimes play on the computer together

h. When the weather is good, my little sister and I watch cartoons together

4. Spot and correct the errors

a. 篮**球**　b. **电影**　c. **有**时**候**　d. **滑板**　e. **一**起　f. **我常常**

5. Complete with: 看, 打 **or** 玩

a. **玩**电脑　b. **打**羽毛球　c. **看**电影　d. **玩**滑板　e. **打**篮球

6. Faulty translation – spot any translation errors and fix them

a. ~~I~~ **We** often play ball games　b. I play ~~tennis~~ **basketball** often　c. I **rarely** go swimming ~~everyday~~

d. When the weather is nice ~~he~~ **we** play~~s~~ with a skateboard　e. I play basketball ~~every week~~ **everyday**

f. I ~~often~~ **rarely** read the newspaper

Unit 14. Free time: READING (Page 153)

1. Highlight the Chinese for the following in Makiyah's text

a. 喜欢打球　b. 和朋友一起 c. 我最喜欢打篮球　d. 可是我的朋友觉得　e. 天气不好的时候

f. 我玩电脑　g. 或者　h. 小说

2. Highlight the Chinese for the following in 义文's text

a. 爱打羽毛球　b. 和我的朋友一起　c. 有时候　d. 滑板　e. 或者　f. 一个星期两次

g. 和我的朋友 Jamie

3. Complete the following statements about Yong Yue

a. She is **Chinese**　b. She is a very **friendly** and **fun** person

THE LANGUAGE GYM

c. She prefers to read books, watch TV or **play on the computer**

d. When the weather is nice she likes to go **to the seaside**

e. She sometimes swims with her **older brother**

4. List 8 details about Olivia (accept answers in any order)

1. She is British   2. When the weather is good, she likes to read books or newspapers in the park

3. She likes to watch cartoons   4. She does not like to play ball games that much

5. She plays badminton sometimes   6. When the weather is good, she goes with her dog to climb a mountain   7. Her dog is called Banjo   8. Her dog is white and brown

9. Her dog is extremely cute and friendly   10. Her dog is her best friend

5. Find someone who…

a. Olivia, Makiyah   b. Yong Yue   c. Makiyah, 义文 Yiwen   d. 义文 Yiwen   e. 义文 Yiwen

Unit 14. Free time: TRANSLATION (Page 154)

1. Gapped translation

a. 我不看小说 - I **don't** read novels   b. 我常常打球 - I often play **ball games**

c. 我有时候打网球 - I **sometimes** play tennis   d. 我**很少**看报 - I rarely read newspapers

e. 我**常常**打篮球 - I often play basketball   f. 我每天玩滑板 - I **skateboard** everyday

g. 天气好的时候，我去骑马 - **When the weather is good**, I go horseriding

2. Translate to English

a. hardly ever/rarely   b. sometimes   c. when the is weather is bad   d. My grandma and I (together)

e. everyday   f. every week   g. Today I want to play basketball   h. I want to read a book

i. I often read novels

3. Translate into English

a. I rarely watch TV with my dad   b. My younger brother and I skateboard together

c. When the weather is good, my mum and I play basketball together

d. The day after tomorrow my friend and I are going to play on the computer

e. I often watch movies with grandmother

4. Convert into Chinese characters

a. 天气好   b. 羽毛球   c. 一起   d. 我们玩   e. 看电视   f. 看报纸   g. 小说   h. 每天

5. Translate into Chinese

Easier: a. 我很少看书   b. 我常常看小说   c. 有时候，我们看电视   d. 他们星期六打球

Challenge: a. 天气不好的时候，我看电影   b. 天气好的时候，我去游泳

c. 星期天，我去公园遛狗   d. 我喜欢和叔叔一起玩电脑

Unit 14. Free time: WRITING (Page 155)

1. Split sentences

我每个**星期都打球**   我玩电脑，**也打球**   爷爷很**少看电视**   天气好**的时候**   我有时**候喝咖啡**

我常常看**电影**　我每天**都打羽毛球**　弟弟和奶奶**一起玩电脑**

2. Complete the sentences

a. 我喜欢玩**电**脑　b. 我姐姐每**天**都**看**报纸　c. 天气好**的**时候，我**打**篮球　d. 我跟爷爷**一起**喝茶

e. 我**玩**滑板，也**打**羽毛球　f. 我**和/跟**朋友**一**起打球

3. Spot and correct mistakes [note: in some cases a character is missing]

a. 我每**天**都玩滑板　b. 我今**天**要和哥哥一**起**打篮球　c. 我每个**星**期跟朋友一起看电影

d. 我**有**时候看小说　e. 爸爸**和**爷爷一起看报纸　f. 天气不好时候

4. Missing radicals. Complete the character

a. 我**打**篮**球**　b. 我看**动**画片　c. 我**玩**滑板　d. 我看报**纸**　e. 我**打羽毛球**

5. Write a paragraph for each of the people below in the first person singular (I):

Janice: 我叫 Janice。我爱玩电脑。我每天和儿子一起玩电脑，因为很好玩。

Mairi: 我叫 Mairi。我喜欢看小说。我常常和朋友一起看小说，因为很有意思。

Kiyomi: 我叫 Kiyomi。 我很喜欢打球。天气好的时候，我和我的女儿一起打球。我觉得打球比看书好玩。

Grammar Time 13: Drills (Page 157)

1. Match up

每个星期 - **Every week**　每个星期天 - **Every Sunday**　每个周末 - **Every weekend**

每个月 - **Every month**　每次 – **Every time**　每天 – **Every day**

2. Complete with the missing character(s)

a. 每**次**　b. 每**个星**期　c. 每**个**周**末**　d. 每个**月**　e.每**几天**　f. **每个**星期天

3. Spot and correct the translation errors

a. 我每个星期六都去公园 – ~~You~~ I go to the ~~seaside~~ **park** ~~everyday~~ **every Saturday**

b. 我们每个星期天都去海边 - We go to the ~~mountains~~ **seaside** ~~on~~ **every** Sunday~~s~~

c. 我的奶奶每次都喝茶 - My ~~mum~~ **grandma** drinks tea every time

d. 我哥哥每天都吃早饭 - My ~~younger~~ **older** brother eats breakfast everyday

e. 他们每两天都吃打羽毛球 ~~We~~ **They** play ~~basketball~~ **badminton** every two days

f. 我们每次都去她家 ~~They~~ **We** go to ~~grandpa's~~ **her** house every ~~weekend~~ **time**

4. Translate into English

a. We play basketball every day　b. She and the little dog/puppy go to the park every day

c. He and his older sister go to the movies every week　d. Grandpa climbs mountains every month

e. Grandma goes swimming every week　f. They eat seafood every Friday

5. Translate into Chinese

a. 我们每天都去公园　b. 他们每个周末都喝茶　c. 她每天都打篮球　d. 我每个星期六都去跑步

e. 我和妈妈每个周末都去海边　f.我和爸爸每个星期天都打球　g. 我每个星期都去朋友家

h. 他们每个星期三都看电视　i. 我和奶奶每个星期天都看电影　j. 晚饭的时候，他们每次都喝水

Unit 15 - Talking about weather and free time

Grammar Time 14: Saying where and when you do activities with 在 and 去

Revision Quickie 4: Clothes / Free time / Weather

Question Skills 3: Clothes / Free time / Weather

Unit 15. Talking about weather and free time VOCABULARY BUILDING 1 (Page 162)

1. Match up

天气热的时候 – **When it's hot**　天气冷的时候 – **When it's cold**　晴天的时候 – **When it's sunny**

多云的时候 – **When it's cloudy**　天气不好的时候 – **When the weather is bad**

下雨的时候 – **When it's raining**

2. Translate into English

a. When it's cold　b. When the sky is clear　c. When it's cloudy　d. When it is overcast

e. When it snows　f. When the weather is good　g. When the weather is bad

h. When there is free time

3. Complete with the missing word

a. 天气不好的**时**候　b. 天气**冷**的时候　c. **晴**天的时候　d. 阴**天**的时候，我在家里看书

e. 天气好的时**候**，我去公园遛狗　f. 下**雪**的时候，我去山区滑雪

4. Character Jumble [weather]

a. 下雪的时候　b. 下雨的时候　c. 阴天的时候　d. 晴天的时候　e. 天气热的时候　f. 天蓝的时候

g. 有风的时候　h. 多云的候时

5. Associations – match each weather word below with the clothes/activities in the box

1. 天气不好的时候: 穿大衣、在家听音乐、看电视剧、

2. 天气好的时候: 去游泳、去海边、穿高跟鞋、戴帽子、去爬山、踢足球、穿泳衣

3. 下雪的时候: 穿大衣、去滑雪、戴帽子、穿雨衣

6. Complete with a suitable character

a. 天气**好**　b. 我**在**家　c. 下**雨**的时候　d. 我**喜欢**天气热的时候　e. 我去**海边**

Unit 15. Talking about weather and free time VOCABULARY BUILDING 2 (Page 163)

1. Match up

我踢足球 – **I play football**　他们去农村 – **They go to the countryside**

哥哥听音乐 – **Big brother listens to music**　我们去山区 – **We go to the mountains**

爸爸钓鱼 – **Dad goes fishing**

2. Complete with the missing word

a. 我的朋友去**海边**玩　b. 我去**朋友**家　c. 有**时候**我去体育馆　d. 我每个星**期天**在操场跑步

e. 我喜欢**周末**，因为我可以和我的朋友一起出去玩

3. Translate into English

a. My friend's house   b. swimming   c. sunny   d. to climb a mountain   e. skiing

4. Character Jumble [free time activities]

a.去山区爬山   b.去河边钓鱼   c.去农村拍照   d.去公园遛狗   e.去电影院看电影

f.去家朋友看电视剧   g.去游泳馆游泳   h.去海边弹吉他

5. Broken pinyin

a. wǒ / hé / péng yǒu / tī / zú qiú   b. wǒ / āyí / xǐ huan / liù / gǒu   c. wǒ qù péng yǒu jiā

d. Joe / qù / tǐ yù guǎn   e. wǒ / qù / shān qū / pāi zhào   f. wǒ / qù / yóu yǒng guǎn / yóu yǒng

6. Complete with a suitable character

a. 我喜欢滑<u>雪</u>   b. 他去<u>朋</u>友家   c. 他踢<u>足</u>球   d. 我去公<u>园</u>   e. 我<u>去</u>游泳馆

Unit 15. Talking about weather and free time: READING (Page 164)

1. Highlight the Chinese for the following in 大中's text

a. 我是香港人   b. 我是学生   c. 我住在   e. 的时候   f. 天气热   g. 去公园   h. 遛狗

i. 黑色的，也比较小   j. 泳裤

2. Highlight the Chinese for the following in 小雪's text

a. 天蓝的时候   b. 去游泳馆游泳   c. 有时候   d. 去河边钓鱼   e. 有点无聊   f. 出去玩的时候

g. 穿 T 恤   h. 总是   i. 听音乐

3. Complete the following statements about 小雨's text

a. She lives in **the US**   b. She really likes buying **T-shirts** and **jackets**

c. She loves **rainy** days

d. When it's a **rainy** day, she can play on the **computer** with her **older** sister

e. She does not like **cold** weather

f. Her **bird** can speak Chinese

4. Answer in Chinese the questions below about Laura

a.她住在澳大利亚   b.她十四岁   c.有空的时候，她喜欢和朋友一起弹吉他

d.她最喜欢的电影是《冰岛奇缘2》   e.下雪的时候，她去城市玩   f.他不喜欢热天气

5. Find someone who

a. 小雪   b. 小雪   c. Laura   d. 小雨   e. 小雨   f. 小雪   g. 大中   h. Laura   i. Laura

Unit 15. Talking about weather and free time: WRITING (Page 165)

1. Split sentences

天气热的时候**我去海边游泳**   我不喜欢**天气冷的时候**   有风的时候**我穿风衣**   天气冷的时候**我穿毛衣**

下雨的时候，**我穿雨衣**   天气不好的时候，**我在家看书**   天气好的时候，**我去公园**

下雪的时候，**我去山区滑雪**

2. Complete with the correct option

a. 我非常**不喜欢**天气热的时候！　b. **有**风的时候，我在家**听**音乐。

c. 天气**热**的时候，我**去**海边。　d. 有**空**的时候，我在公园踢**足**球。

3. Spot and correct the grammar and spelling mistakes [note: in several cases a character is missing]

a. 有腔**空**的时候，我去朋家看电视剧。　b. 天绿**蓝**的时~~猴~~**候**，我要去操场踢足球。

c. 多运**云**的时候，我不相**想**去海边拍照。　d. 晴天好的时候，我的朋友要去山凶**区**爬山。

e. 有凤**风**的时候，我想**在**家看电景**影**。　f. 周末的时候，我要去胡**湖**边钓鱼。

g. ~~丹~~**阴**天的时候，我特别不想去农村留**遛**狗。

4. Complete the pinyin to Chinese characters

a. a. fēng – 风　b. xuě – 雪　c. lěng – 冷　d. rè – 热

5. Guided writing – write 3 short paragraphs in the first person [I] using the details below

Ellie: 我叫 Ellie。我住在英国。天气好的时候，我和朋友一起去公园玩。

Santi: 我叫 Santi，我住在中国。天气热和晴天的时候，我和我的狗一起去海边。

Juliet: 我叫 Juliet。我住在美国。天气冷和下雨的时候，我和我姐姐的狗一起看电影。

6. Describe this person in Chinese using the 3rd person [she]

她叫 Paula，她住在美国的西部。她十三岁，有一只白色的狗。晴天的时候，她总是去公园打球。她不喜欢在家看电视。

Grammar Time 14: Saying where and when you do activities with 在 and 去 (Page 167)

1. Complete with the one of the following characters for places: 院 – 场 – 馆 – 海 – 区 – 边

a. 电影**院**　b. 医**院**　c. 游泳**馆**　d. 山**区**　e. 操**场**　f. 饭**馆**　g. **海**边　h. 湖**边**　i. 体育**馆**

2. Spot the grammar and character errors

a. 我**星期五**要去公园遛狗。　b. 我阿姨每个月都**去农村**拍照。　c. 我妈妈~~海~~**每**天都去~~海~~**海**边。

d. 我女儿不想去操场炮**跑**步。　e. 我孙女儿很~~小~~**少**在家看电影。

f. 我孙子有时候在**体**体育馆易**踢**是**足**球。　g. 我男朋友和我**常常**一起在朋友家玩。

3. Translate into English

a. I want to go to the cinema to watch a film on Monday.

b. At the weekends, my friend takes photos in the mountains.

c. Every month, my father goes to the countryside to walk the dog.

d. My uncle goes fishing in the lake every day.

e. My son wants to swim at the seaside every week.

f. I am going to a restaurant to have dinner tomorrow.

4. Complete with a suitable time word

a. 我**星期**四在游泳馆游泳。　b. 我妈妈**常**常和朋友一起去饭馆吃饭。

c. 我**周**末是在体育馆踢足球。　d. 我后**天**不在。　e. 有**时**候，我去农村遛狗。

5. Translate into Chinese

a. 我总是在电影院看电影　b. 我妈妈常常在湖边看书　c. 周末的时候，我哥哥喜欢去山区

d. 哥哥和我每天都在公园打篮球

Revision Quickie 4: Clothes/Free time/Weather (Page 168)

1. Activities -Match

我去操场 – **I go to the playground**　我去健身房 – **I go to the gym**　我去湖边 – **I go to the lakeside**

我游泳 – **I go swimming**　我踢足球 – **I play football**　我吃饭 – **I eat food**

我去饭馆 – **I go to the restaurant**　我拍照 – **I take photos**　我弹吉他 – **I play guitar**

我去河边 – **I go to the riverside**

2. Weather – Complete

a. 执 = 热　b. 令 = 冷　c. 厶 = 云　d. 青 = 晴　e. ヨ = 雪　f. 月天 = 阴天

3. Fill in the gaps in Chinese

a. 天气**冷**的时候，我**穿大衣**　b. 天气不好的时**候**，我**看书**　c. 晴天的**时候**，我去海边

d. **在**健饭馆的时**候**，我**吃**高兴　e. 有**空**的时**候**，我踢**足球**

4. Translate into Chinese (easier)

a. 天气热的时候　b. 天气冷的时候　c. 我打球　d. 有空的时候　e. 我听音乐　f. 下雨的时候

g. 我去海边　h. 我去电影院

5. Translate to Chinese (challenge)

a. 我穿大衣　b. 我们穿鞋子　c. 他们打篮球　d. 她去爬山　e. 他没有空　f. 他们去游泳

g. 我爸爸妈妈不喜欢钓鱼　h. 她常常在饭馆吃饭

Question Skills 3: Drills (Page 172)

1. Translate into English

a. When the weather is cold, what kind of clothes do you wear?　b. How's the weather today?

c. When there is free time, what do you like to do?　d. Do you play basketball often?

e. Why don't you like to play football?　f. When do you go to China?

h. How many times a week do you go to your friend's house?

2. Complete with the missing question word

a. 你为**什么**不喜欢天气热的时候？　b. 中国天气**怎么样**？　c. 你喜欢穿什么**样**的衣服？

d. 你常常弹吉他**吗**？　e. 你**什么时候**去？　f. 你每个月去农村几**次**？

3. Split questions

你什么**时候去法国？**　天气热的**时候，你戴帽子吗？**　有空的时候，你喜欢做什么？

你为什么**不喜欢看书？**　你常常**去电影院吗？**　你每个星**期去体育馆几次？**

你喜欢**穿什么样的衣服？**

4. Translate into Chinese

a. 什么？ b. 在哪儿？　c. 怎么样？　d. 什么时候？　e. 还是？　f. 你多大？　g. 你几岁？

h. 你常常…吗？　i. 哪一个？

5. Write the questions to these answers

a. 天气冷的时候，你穿什么样的衣服？

b. 周末的时候，你做什么？/ 你什么时候和朋友一起出去玩？　c. 你什么时候去健身房？

d. 你喜欢什么颜色的帽子和鞋子？　e. 你常常去爬山吗？　f. 你为什么喜欢去饭馆吃饭？

6. Translate into Chinese

a. 你为什么喜欢去饭馆？　b. 有空的时候，你喜欢做什么？　c. 你每个星期去公园几次？

d. 周末的时候，你喜欢穿什么样的衣服？　e. 你什么时候看电视？

Unit 16 - Talking about my daily routine

Revision Quickie 5: Clothes / Food / Free time / Describing People

Unit 16. Talking about my daily routine: VOCAB BUILDING (Part 1) (Page 178)

1. Match up

我回家 – **I go back home**　我起床 – **I get up**　我睡觉 – **I sleep**　我吃午饭 – **I have lunch**

我上学 – **I start school**　我吃晚饭 – **I have dinner**　我休息一会儿 – **I rest for a while**

我吃早饭 – **I have breakfast**

2. Translate into English

a. I get up at 6am　b. I go to sleep at 11pm　c. I have lunch at noon　d. I go back home at 3.30pm or so

e. I have dinner at 7pm or so　f. I watch TV at 8.30pm every evening　g. I listen to music at 10.20am

3. Complete with the missing words

a. 我<u>上</u>学　b. 我<u>做</u>作业　c. 我<u>回</u>家　d. 我看<u>电</u>视　e. 我听音<u>乐</u>　f. 我<u>玩</u>电脑　g.我吃<u>早</u>饭

h. 中<u>午</u>十二点　i. 晚上八<u>点</u>左右　j. 早上六点二十<u>五</u><u>分</u>左右

4. Faulty translation – spot and correct any translation mistakes. Not all translations are wrong.

a. I get up at 6.30am　**CORRECT**　b. I go to sleep at noon　**CORRECT**　c. I do ~~your~~ homework

d. I have dinner at **5:30pm or so**　e. At ~~7.10am~~ **7:20am every morning**, I ~~often~~ have breakfast

f. At ~~7pm~~ **8pm** or so, I ~~play on my phone~~ **give a friend a call**

g. At around 7:10am, I take the bus to school　**CORRECT**

5. Translate the following times into Chinese

a. 早上六点半/早上六点三十分　b. 早上七点三十五分　c.晚上八点二十分　d. 中午十二点

e. 上午九点二十七分　f. 晚上十一点　g. 下午两点四十五分左右　h. 晚上九点十三分

i. 早上六点左右

Unit 16. Talking about my daily routine: VOCABULARY BUILDING (Part 2) (Page 179)

1. Complete the table

早上六点左右 – **About 6am**　**我起床** – I get up　我玩电脑 – **I play on the computer**

我回家 – I go back home　我睡觉 – **I go to sleep**　我吃午饭 – **I have lunch**

我吃晚饭 – I have dinner　我听音乐 – **I listen to music**　**我看电视** – I watch TV

我吃早饭 – **I have breakfast**　我休息一会儿 – **I rest for a while**　**我做作业** – I do homework

2. Complete the sentences using the words in the table below

a. 七<u>点</u>三十分　b. <u>五</u>点左<u>右</u>　c. <u>早</u>上八点　d. <u>下</u><u>午</u>三点　e. 十一点十<u>五</u><u>分</u>　f. 两点四十分<u>左</u><u>右</u>

3. Translate into English (numerical)

a. 8.30　b. 2.00　c. 11.11am　d. 12.00　e. 1.05　f. 10.55　g. 4.50

4. Add the missing tone marks

a. zuò zuò yè　b. shuì jiào　c. xiū xi yí huìr　d. gěi péng you dǎ diàn huà　e. qù xué xiào

f. zuò gōng gòng qì chē   g. huí jiā   h. zǎo shang wǔ diǎn shí fēn   i. xià wǔ liǎng diǎn bàn zuǒ yòu

5. Translate the following into Chinese

a. 早上八点左右，我上学   b. 下午三点左右，我回家   c. 晚上七点半/七点三十分，我吃晚饭

d. 下午五点半/五点三十分左右，我做作业   e. 早上六点四十五分，我吃早饭

f. 晚上十一点五十分，我睡觉

Unit 16. Talking about my daily routine: READING (Part 1) (Page 180)

1. Answer the following questions about Hiro

a. Chinese   b. At around 6am   c. With his younger brother   d. At around 7.30am

e. Until around 7 pm   f. By bus   g. He eats dinner (then watches TV)

2. Find the Chinese for the following phrases/sentences in Gregory's text

a. 我是法国人   b. 我是医生   c. 和我儿子   d. 我休息一会儿   e. 我吃米饭或者沙拉   f. 我听音乐

g. 晚饭的时候   h. 十一点半

3. Complete the statements below about Jurgen

a. He gets up at **around 5am**   b. He leaves work at **around 5.20pm** to go home   c. For breakfast he

eats **fruit salad and bread**   d. He has breakfast with **his mother**   e. After getting up he **goes jogging**

and then he has breakfast   f. At **6pm**, he watches **TV**, he often watches **football**

Unit 16. Talking about my daily routine: READING (Part 2) (Page 181)

1. Highlight the Chinese for the following in Yang's text

a. 我是台湾人   b. 每天早上   c. 起床   d. 六点半左右   e. 七点半   f. 我们常常   g. 听音乐

h. 去学校   i. 我做作业   j. 最后，晚上十一点四十五分左右

2. Translate these items from Kim's text

a. 我是英国人   b. 我们总是   c. 每天早上五点三十分左右   d. 和妹妹一起   e. 我回家

f. 下午三点左右   g. 我和家人一起吃晚饭   h. 我们常常吃很多

3. Answer the following questions on Anna's text

a. Scottish   b. around 7.15 am   c. She has a rest, has something to eat, watches TV or reads a novel

d. by bus   e. with her older sister   f. at around 11pm   g. seafood or noodles   h. reads a book

4. Find Someone who…

a. Anna   b. Anna   c. Anna   d. Kim   e. Yang.   f. Anna, Kim, Yang   g. Kim

Unit 16. Talking about my daily routine: WRITING (Page 182)

1. Split sentences

每天早上我去学校   每天早上六**点，我起床**   下午三点零**五左右**   我看**电视，然后睡觉**

八点十分左**右，我吃晚饭**   我给朋友**打电话**   我早上七点吃**早饭**   每天下午两点**半左右，我回家**

2. Complete with the correct option

a 每天下**午**两**点**左右   b. 早上七**点**零五分，我起床   c. 每天下**午**三点**左**右   d. 我晚**上**六点**做**作业

e. 我坐公共汽车去**学**校

3. Spot and correct the grammar and spelling mistakes [in several cases a word is missing]

a. 我坐公共汽车**去**学校　b. 早上七半，我起床　c. **晚上**八点晚上，我回家

d. 我星期~~二~~**两**点去朋友家　e. ~~左右~~下午三点**左右**，我休息一会儿

f. ~~每天我睡觉~~十一点左右，**我睡觉**

4. Rewrite the sentences in the correct order

a. 十一点半　b. 一点左右　c. 晚上七点四十五分　d. 早上五点三十分　e. 八点十五分左右

f. 每天上午十点十五分

5. Guided writing – write 3 short paragraphs in the first person [I] using the details below

Eleanor: 我叫 Eleanor。每天早上六点半，我起床。我七点吃早饭。我八点零五分上学。下午三点半，我回家。晚上六点，我看电视。八点十分，我吃晚饭。晚上十一点十分，我睡觉。

Molly: 我叫 Molly。早上六点四十分，我起床。早上七点十分，我吃早饭。七点四十分，我上学。下午四点，我回家。晚上六点半，我看电视。八点十五分，我吃晚饭。晚上十点，我睡觉。

Martha: 我叫 Martha。早上起点十五分，我起床。早上七点半，我吃早饭。我八点上学。下午三点十五分，我回家。晚上六点四十五分，我看电视。八点二十分，我吃晚饭。晚上十一点半，我睡觉。

Revision Quickie 5: Clothes/Food/Free Time/Describing people (Page 183-184)

1. Clothes – Match up

雨衣 – **raincoat**　帽子 – **hat**　袜子 – **socks**　裤子 – **trousers**　领带 – **tie**　手表 – **watch**

大衣 – **coat**　裙子 – **skirt**　T恤 – **t-shirt**　衬衣 – **shirt**

2. Food – Provide a word for the pinyin cues below

A fruit starting with **P – píngguǒ**　A colour starting with **H – hóngsè / huángsè / huīsè**

A clothing item starting with **K – kùzi**　A meat starting with **N – niúròu**

A drink starting with **Q – qìshuǐ**　A drink starting with **C – chá**　A colour starting with **F – fěnhóngsè**

3. Spot and coorect the errors

a. Shoes - **鞋子**　b. Hat - **帽子**　c. Hair - 头**发**　d. Clever - **聪**明　e. Purple - 紫**色**　f. Milk - **牛奶**

4. Clothes, Colours, Food, Jobs – Categories

Clothes: 大衣、袜子、衬衣、领带　**Colours:** 蓝色、粉红色、红色　**Work:** 护士、司机、工人

Food: 桔子、肉、饺子、面条、鸡肉

5. Match questions and answers

a. 你喜欢什么颜色？ - **3. 蓝色**　b. 你吃猪肉吗？ - **6. 不吃**　c. 你要喝茶还是咖啡？ - **1. 喝茶**

d. 他高吗？ - **7. 非常高**　e. 你喜欢看书吗？ - **2. 喜欢**　f. 你的老师人怎么样？ - **5. 很友好**

g. 你要穿哪一个，裤子还是裙子？ - **4. 裤子**

6. (Free time) Complete with 玩、打、看、去 as appropriate

a. 我每天都**打**篮球　b. 我爱**玩**滑板，也爱**打**羽毛球　c. 我下午一点**去**公园，两点**回**家

d. 我**看**小说，也**看**动画片

7. Complete with the missing verb, choosing from the list below

a. 我每天都**喝**果汁。　b. 我们**吃**饺子。　c. 我**有**黑色的头发。　d. 我爸爸**穿**红色的衬衣。

e. 我不**看**电视，也不**听**音乐。　f. 他**是**中国人，不**是**英国人。

8. Time markers – Translate

a. 常常 – often　b. 总是 – always　c. 每天 – everyday　d. 很少 - rarely　e. 每次 - everytime

9. Split sentences (Relationships)

我爱我**奶奶**　我和**弟弟关系好**　因为我妈**妈很友好**　我的男朋**友非常大方**

我妈妈和爸爸**都很亲切**　我和她的关**系不好**　我妹妹很可爱，**也很好玩**

我不喜欢他，　因**为他很烦人**

10. Translate into Chinese

a. 我每天都打球　b. 有时候，我穿大衣/夹克　c. 我常常去公园　d. 我不看电视

e. 早上六点左右，我起床　f. 我和奶奶一起听音乐

11. Complete the translation

a. 我哥哥是老**师**　b. 我没有**工**作，因为我是学**生**

c. 天气好的的**时**候，我和爸爸**一起**打篮球　d. 我很**少**看**电**视　e. 我**不**喜欢穿大**衣**

Unit 17 - Describing my house

Grammar Time 15: Describing where something is (1)

Unit 17. Describing my house: VOCAB BUILDING (PART 1) (Page 190)

1. Match up

我住在 - **I live in**   房子 - **house**   卧室 - **bedroom**   城市 - **city**   郊区 - **outskirts**

农村 - **countryside**   大 – **big**

2. Translate into English

a. I live on the beautiful outskirts   b. My house is extremely big   c. I live in a boring small town

d. My house is in the countryside   e. My house has two bedrooms   f. I like my aunt's kitchen

g. I like resting in the living room   h. Grandma is always playing with her mobile phone in the toilet

3. Complete with the missing words

a. 我住在**海边** b. 我喜欢我的**房子** c. 我住在一个**美丽**的小镇 d. 我经常在**客厅**休息

4. Write the characters (about '我的房子')

a. 城市   b. 有意思   d. 饭厅

5. Classify the words/phrases below in the table below

Time phrases: a, n   **Nouns:** e, f, g, k, m   **Verbs:** b, j   **Adjectives:** c, d, h, i, l

6. Translate into Chinese

a. 我的房子很大   b. 我住在一个有意思的城市   c. 我常常在客厅里看书

d. 我喜欢在花园里休息一会   e. 我总是在饭厅里玩手机   f. 中午的时候，爸爸在书房里工作

Unit 17. Describing my house: VOCABULARY BUILDING (PART 2) (Page 191)

1. Match up

在花园里 - **in the garden**   我经常 - **I often**   我最喜欢 - **I most like**   在厕所里 - **in the toilet**

在厨房里 - **in the kitchen**   我很少 **I rarely**   我总是 - **I always**

2. Complete with the missing word

a. 我不**喜**欢做作业   b. 我的房子不大，**但是/可是**很漂亮   c. 在**农村**   d. 在**客厅里**

e. 我的**房子**很大

3. Translate into English

a. My house is not big   b. It is on the coast/by the sea   c. Ugly big house   d. On the outskirts   e. There are five bedrooms in my house   f. I like to work in the dining room   g. I like to relax   h. My home is by the sea/on the coast   i. I like my bedroom

4. Broken pinyin

a. wǒ / xǐ h**uān** / xiū x**i**   b. w**ǒ** / zhù z**ài** / sh**ān** qū   c. y**í** / ge / xi**ǎo** zh**èn**   d. w**ǒ** / zǒng sh**ì** / w**án** sh**ǒu** jī

e. z**ài** / h**uā** yu**án** / l**ǐ**   f. w**ǒ** / z**uì** / xǐ h**uān**

5. 厅, 室, 园 or 房?

a. 书**房**   b. 卧**室**   c. 厨**房**   d. 花**园**   e. 饭**厅**

6. Faulty translation – spot any translation errors and fix them

a. I live on the ~~French~~ **British** coast   b. I most like to ~~relax~~ **play on my mobile phone** in the ~~dining~~
living room   c. I like to ~~do my homework~~ **listen to music** in ~~my bedroom~~ **the dining room**
d. My house is ~~in a city~~ **on the outskirts**   e. I ~~don't~~ like my house because it is **extremely** big ~~ugly~~
f. I ~~often~~ **rarely** work in the ~~study~~ **kitchen**   g. My house has 3 ~~bedrooms~~ **bathrooms**

Unit 17. Describing my house: READING (Page 192)

1. Answer the following questions about 小月

a. Chinese   b. She thinks it's interesting and likes it c. Not big   d. She likes to play on her phone
e. In the living room   f. In the beautiful countryside   g. He is humorous and friendly

2. Highlight the Chinese for the phrases below in 大卫's text

a. 我住在一个没意思的小镇   b. 坐公共汽车去   c. 但是在学校   d. 我们家也有一个美丽的花园
e. 我爱吃   f. 经常在花园里跑   g. 睡觉或者玩电脑

3. Find Someone Who...

a. Ariel   b. 大卫   c. 大卫   d. Jason   e. 大卫   f. Ariel   g. 大卫   h. 小月

4. Find the Chinese for the following phrases/sentences in Ariel's text

a. 我是美国人   b. 我总是早上五点起床   c. 我的学校在城市里   d. 我的房子很老
e. …也有一点丑   f. 可是我喜欢

Unit 17. Describing my house: TRANSLATION (Page 193)

1. Gapped translation

a. 我住在郊区 - I live on the **outskirts**

b. 我的房子很大，但是有一点丑 - My house is **very** big but **a bit** ugly

c. 在山区 - It is in the **mountains**   d. 我住在**城市** - I live in the city

e. 我的**房子**两个卧室 - My house has two bedrooms

2. Translate to English

a. the seaside   b. house   c. city   d. countryside   e. I often   f. I like to relax   g. my bedroom
h. in the living room

3. Translate into English

a. I live in a quite ugly little house   b. My house is not old   c. My house is very old, but I like it a lot
d. I live by the sea in China   e. My house has four bedrooms
f. I like playing on my mobile phone in the study the most

4. Translate into Chinese

a. Big - **大**   b. Small – **小**   c. Outskirts - 郊**区**   d. Coast – **海**边   e. Bedroom - 卧**室**

5. Translate into Chinese

a. 我住在一个很大的房子 b. 在城市里 c. 我的房子里有… d. 两个卧室

e. 我经常和我的狗在花园里玩 f. 在饭厅里 g. 我喜欢在客厅里休息 h. 我也喜欢在书房里工作

i. 我的房子比较旧 j. 在海边

Grammar Time 15: Drills (Page 196)

1. Match

外面 – **outside** 中间 – **between** 对面 – **opposite** 前面 - **in front of** 左边 – **left** 后面 - **behind**

2. Complete with the correct location word

a. 厨房在客厅**前面** b. 饭厅在书房**右边** c. 姐姐的卧室在我的卧室**对面** d. 浴室在你**左边**

e. 妈妈要坐在爸爸和爷爷的**中间** f. 花园在房子**后面**

3. Complete the translation

a. Dad is outside - 爸爸在**外面** b. I am inside the house - 我在房子**里面**

c. He lives between Beijing and Oxford - 他住在北京和天津**中间**

d. **Who** is that beside you? - **谁**在你**旁边** e. The company is opposite the school - 公司在学校**对面**

f. The hospital is to the right of the supermarket - 医院在超市**右边**

g. The mountains are outside the city - 山区在城市**外边**

h. My home is between my aunt and grandma's - 我家在阿姨和奶奶家**中间**

4. Spot and correct the errors

a. 客厅是在我旁边 b. **厕所在**花园在厕所里 c. 书房子在浴室对面 d. 我在厨房前面条

e. 卧**我**在我是**卧室**里边

5. Translate into Chinese

a. 我的狗在外面 b. 客厅在饭厅前边 c. 我爷爷奶奶住在我朋友和我爸爸的房子中间

d. 书房在爸爸妈妈的卧室对面 e. 花园在房子后面

Unit 18 - Saying what I do at home
Grammar Time 16: Describing where something is (2)

Unit 18. Saying what I do at home: VOCAB BUILDING (Part 1) (Page 202)

1. Match up

我穿好衣服 - **I get dressed**   我和妈妈聊天 - **I chat with mum**   我看电影 - **I watch movies**

我做饭 - **I make food**   我做作业 - **I do homework**   我看杂志 - **I read magazines**

我看漫画 - **I read comics**

2. Complete with the missing words

a. 我穿好**衣服**   b. 我爱看**漫画书**   c. 我**做**作业   d. 我和爸爸**聊天**

3. Translate into English

a. I usually get up at around 7 in the morning   b. I never make food

c. I usually read magazines in the living room

d. At around 7:30am I have breakfast in the dining room

e. I sometimes chat with mum in the kitchen

f. I sometimes play on the PS4/5 with my little brother in the bedroom

g. I sometimes have breakfast in the kitchen   h. I always go to school at around 8am

i. I often read comics in my older sister's room

4. Rewrite the characters so they include their missing parts

a. 起**床**   b. **看**书   c. **聊**天   d. **做**   e. 电**影**   f. 衣服   g. **玩**   h. 电视**剧**   i. 上网   j. 休**息**

5. Classify the words/phrases below in the table below

Time phrases: a, b, c, i, k, n

Rooms in the house: d

Things you do in the bathroom: g, k, m

Free-time activities: e, f, h, k, m

6. Fill the gaps to indicate which room the activity is done in

玩 PS 四/五 - 卧**室**

看电视 – 客**厅**

做饭 – 厨**房**

看书 - 书**房**

踢足球 – 花**园**

Unit 18. Saying what I do at home: VOCABULARY BUILDING (Part 2) (Page 203)

7. Complete the table

I get dressed - **我穿好衣服**   I get up - **我起床**   I do homework - 我作业   I watch TV - **我看电视**

I go to a friend's house - 我去朋友家   **I chat with my younger brother** - 我和弟弟聊天

I rest - **我休息一会儿**

8. Multiple choice quiz

从来不 - **B never**　　有时候 – **A sometimes**　　卧室 - **A bedroom**　　穿好衣服 – **B get dressed**

我休息 - **C I rest**　　我看书 - **A I read**　　花园 - **A garden**　　厨房 - **C kitchen**　　我做 – **C I make**

我玩 - **C I play**　　总是 – **A Always**

9. Character Jumble

a. **有**时候 – sometimes　　b. 我经**常** – I often　　c. 六**点左**右 – at around 6 o'clock

d. **我**每天 – everyday I　　e. **的**时候 – when　　f. 我**一般** – I usually

10. Missing character

a. **厨**房　　b. 从**来**不　　c. 有**时**候　　d. 总**是**　　e. **经/常**常

11. Complete based on the translation in brackets

a. 我早**上**七点半**左**右穿好**衣**服　　b. 我八**点**十分**吃**早饭　　c. 我有**时**候**做**饭

d. 我**吃**早饭的**时**候，看**电**视　　e. 我很**少**看**漫**画**书**

12. Gap-fill from memory

a. 我**有**时候看漫画书。　　b. 我吃早**饭**的时候**总**是看杂志。　　c. 我**每**天都在 Netflix 上看电视**剧**。

d. 我**从**来不**做**作业。

Unit 18. Saying what I do at home: READING (Page 204)

1. Answer the following questions about 曼丽

a. Singaporean　　b. a dog　　c. she gets dressed, then goes to the gym　　d. he does not go to the gym

e. to go out with friends or chat with her dad in the living room

f. he is clever and loves her very much　　g. in her bedroom

2. Highlight the Chinese for the phrases below in Edward's text

a. 起床　　b. 吃早饭　　c. 学校　　d. 坐公共汽车　　e. 骑自行车　　f. 我觉得　　g. 很忙　　h. 很少和我聊天

3. Find Someone Who

a. Edward　　b. Edward　　c. Vicky　　d. Vicky　　e. 曼丽　　f. Vicky　　g. Edward　　h. Vicky

4. Find the Chinese for the following phrases/sentences in Vicky's text

a. 我是香港人　　b. 我总是六点起床　　c. 我从来不吃早饭　　d. 姐姐和我爸爸　　e. 在饭厅里吃烤面包

f. 在客厅里　　g. 在 TikTok 上看幽默的小视频

Unit 18. Saying what I do at home: WRITING (Page 205)

1. Split sentences

我在 Tiktok **上看小视频**　　我在卧**室里**　　我吃**午饭**　　我们在花**园里踢足球**　　我早**上休息**　　我起**床**

我和妈妈**聊天**

63

2. Complete with the correct option

a. 我六点**起**床　b. 我早**上**踢足球　c. 我五点半**看**电视　d. 我和爸爸一起**做**饭

e. 我在 Spotify 上**听**音乐

3. Spot and correct the grammar and spelling mistakes [note: in several cases a word is missing and/added]

a. 我**在浴室里**穿好衣服~~在浴室里~~　b. 我**在**厨房**里**吃早饭　c. 在卧室~~的~~里

d. **在客厅里**玩电脑~~在客厅~~　e. 我八点出去玩~~八点~~　f. 做~~昨~~作业　g. 在 Netflix 上~~吃~~**听**音乐

h. 我哥哥的卧**室**

4. Rewrite the characters so they include their missing parts

a. 我**吃**早饭　b. 在**厨**房里　c. 我的**卧**室　d. 花**园**　e. 我回**家**　f. 在**客**厅里　g. 在**饭**厅里

h. 在**浴**室里　i. 我在哥哥的**卧**室里看**电影**

5. Guided writing – write 3 short paragraphs in the first person [I] using the details below

小月：我叫小月。我早上六点十五分起床。我在厨房里吃早饭。我和哥哥一起去学校。中午十二点，我吃午饭。我晚上喜欢在客厅里看电视或者在厨房里做饭。

大中：我叫大中。我早上七点半/七点三十分起床。我在饭厅里吃早饭。我和妈妈一起去学校。中午十二点半/十二点三十分，我吃午饭。我晚上一般在卧室里看书或者和家人聊天。

东东：我叫东东。我早上六点四十五分起床。我在客厅里吃早饭。我和爸爸一起去学校。下午一点，我吃午饭。我晚上经常在花园里听音乐或者玩手机。

Grammar Time 16: Drills (Page 207)

1. Complete with 上, 下 or 里

a. 电视**上**说今天天气多云　b. 桌子**上/下**有一只猫　c. 书架**上**有一些书　d. 书包**里**有三支红笔

2. Circle the location words that fit most logically with the item in the left column

电视 - **上**　桌子 - **下/上**　书包 - **里**　教室 - **里/外**　卧室 - **里**　厨房 - **外**　YouTube - **上**

椅子 - **下/上**　书房 - **外/里**　房子 - **外**　书架 - **上**

3. Complete with the appropriate location word

a. 我在公园**里**遛狗　b. 我在书房**里**做作业　c. 电视**上**说今天下雨　d. 老师坐在椅子**上**

Unit 19 - My holiday plans

Revision Quickie 6: Daily Routine / House / Home life / Holidays

Question Skills 4: Daily Routine / House / Home life / Holidays

Unit 19. My holiday plans: VOCABULARY BUILDING (Page 213)

1. Match up

度假 - **have a holiday**　我打算 - **I plan to**　我想 - **I would like to**

一定会 - **sure to be**　住在 - **to stay in**　买 - **to buy**　单人房 - **single room**　旅游车 - **coach/tour bus**

2. Complete with the missing word

a. 我要拍**照**　b. 我要**休息**　c. 我**想**去　d. 和朋友一起**玩**　e. 我要住**在**

3. Translate into English

a. When it's the summer holiday, me and my family are planning to go to Germany

 b. I'm going to stay there for 3 weeks　c. I'm going to go to China by plane

d. We would like to go to the shopping centre to buy souvenirs　e. I'd like to go dancing

f. I'm going to play with my friends　g. We would like to visit some museums

h. We would like to sunbathe everyday

4. Rewrite the characters so that they include ther missing components

a. 购**物**中心　b. 我们要**住**在　c. 度**假**　d. 我**想**去　e. 去**海**边

5. Write a suitbale mode of transport according to the gaps given

a. 飞机　b. 汽车/火车　c. 船　d. 自行车

6. Faulty translation – spot any translation errors and fix them

a. When it's the summer holiday, ~~my family and I~~ **we** are going to **go to**…

b. I ~~would like~~ **am planning** to go to America with my mother by ~~train~~ **plane**

c. I am going to take ~~a walk~~ **photos**　d. I would like to rest **everyday**

e. I am staying in a ~~single~~ **double** room　f. I am going to stay there for ~~one week~~ **two weeks**

Unit 19. My holiday plans: READING (Part 1) (Page 214)

1. Highlight the Chinese for the following in Hugo's text

a. 我是　b. 但是我住在　c. 我打算　d. 我和我的男朋友　e. 我们要在那儿住　f. 每天(都)

g. 我不想去　h. 在游泳池旁边晒太阳…

2. Highlight the Chinese for the following in Diana's text

a. 暑假　b. 坐船去　c. 我打算在那儿住　d. 我非常喜欢跳舞　e. 去城市里　f. 应该　g. 非常无聊

"

3. Complete the following statements about John

a. He is **American**   b. The person he likes the most is **Jen/his spouse**   c. They will travel to **Canada** by **tour bus/coach**

d. John would like to rest, **read books** and **ski** and is also planning to see some **friends**

e. Jen is going to **ride a bike** and **eat lots of tasty food**

4. List any 8 details about 小雨 (in 3rd person) in English

1. She is Taiwanese   2. This summer holiday she is going to the UK on her own

4. She is going to spend 2 weeks   6. She is going to go to the seaside

7. She is going to stay in a caravan   8. She is going to visit many museums and buy lots of souvenirs

9. She thinks British Culture is really interesting

5. Find someone who…

a. Diana   b. 小雨   c. Hugo   d. Diana   e. John and Jen

Unit 19. My holiday plans: READING (Part 2) (Page 215)

1. Answer the following questions about 婷婷

a. Chinese   b. a big cat   c. in the eastern part of China (and also Taiwan)   e. in a single room

e. by boat   f. buy clothes

2. Highlight the Chinese for the phrases below in 梦茹's text

a. 暑假   b. 度假   c. 一间双人房   d. 特别漂亮   e. 我们打算   f. 晒太阳   g. 一定会很好玩

h. 工作

3. Find Someone Who

a. 梦茹   b. 梦茹   c. 婷婷   d. 梦茹   e. 婷婷   f. Kiky   g. Kiky   h. Kiky's partner

4. Highlight the Chinese for the following phrases/sentences in Kiky's text

a. 带我儿子   b. 去一个特别的地方   c. 觉得会非常非常好玩   d. 买很多纪念品   e. 水很蓝

f. 我爱人更喜欢   g. 美国队长和绿巨人   g. 应该

Unit 19. My holiday plans: TRANSLATION/WRITING (Page 216)

1. Gapped translation

a.我们要去**度假**   b.我打算**开车**去   c.我们要**在**那儿住一个**星期**   d. 爸爸妈妈要住在一间**双人房**

e. 我们打算在**山区**拍**照**

2. Translate to English

a. buy souvenirs   b. take photos   c. rest   d. coach/tour bus   e. to go to the seaside   f. everyday

g. by plane   h. visit museums   i. sunbathe   j. dance

3. Spot and correct the grammar and spelling mistakes [note: in several cases a word is missing]

a. 我想晒~~夫~~**太**阳   b. 我打算在~~哪~~**那**儿**住**两个星期   c. 我打算**住**在一个单身人房

d. **爸爸**妈妈要去**狗购**物中心   e. 我想踢足**求球**   f. 我们要**去**城市里玩

4. Categories: Positive or Negative?

a. 我觉得应该会很好玩 – **P**   b. 我觉得应该会很无聊 – **N**   c. 我觉得应该会很好的 – **P**

d. 我觉得一定会非常有意思 – **P**   e. 我觉得可能会没意思 – **N**   f. 他一定会喜欢 - **P**

g. 我觉得应该会很累 – **N**   h. 我觉得可能会不好玩 - **N**

5. Translate into Chinese

a. 我要休息   b. 我们打算去度假   c. 我们想要去海边   d. 我们打算坐火车去

e. 我要坐飞机去美国   f. 我要住在   g. 单人房   h. 我们要在那儿住两个星期   i. 我要坐飞机去

j. 我觉得应该会很好玩

Revision Quickie 6: Daily Routine/House/Home life/Holidays (Page 217- 218)

1. Match-up

在花园里 - **In the garden**   在厨房里 - **In the kitchen**   在饭厅里 - **In the dining room**

在客厅里 - **In the living room**   在我的房子里 - **In my house**   在卧室里 - **In my bedroom**

在浴室里 - **In the bathroom**   在书房里 - **In the study**   在郊区 - **On the outskirts**

2. Rewrite the characters so they include their missing parts

a. 我吃早**饭**   b. 我**起**床 c. 我看**电**视   d. 我喜欢看**漫**画   e. 我**回**家   f. 我去**学**校

g. 我**坐**公共**汽**车去

3. Spot and correct any of the sentences below which do not make sense (possible answers)

a. 我在厨房里~~起床~~**做饭**   b. 我在浴室~~饭厅~~里吃东西   c. 我在书房里做~~饭~~**作业**

d. 我在客厅里~~坐火车~~**休息/听音乐/看电视**   e. 我坐公共汽车去我的~~卧室~~**学校**

f. 我和我的狗一起~~吃~~**做**作业   g. 爸爸的~~猫~~开车去德国的农村   h. 我在~~烤鸭~~**客厅**里看电视

i. 我睡在~~太阳~~**卧室**里   j. 我的车在我的~~卧室~~**里上**

4. Split sentences

我爱看**电视**   我喜欢拍**照**   我听**音乐**   我喝**咖啡**   我在**卧室里做作业**   我想去德**国的农村**

我在 Tiktok 上**看小视频**   我打算坐**火车去山区**   我想吃**苹果**   我玩电**脑**

5. Match the opposites

很好 - **不好**   无聊 - **好玩**   容易 - **难**   有意思 - **没意思**   好吃 - **难吃**   丑 - **漂亮**   强 - **弱**

从来不 - **总是**   胖 - **瘦**   小气 - **大方**   高 - **矮**

6. Complete with the missing words

a. 我们**坐**飞机去中国   b. 我从来**不**踢足球   c. 我非常不喜欢**打**篮球   d. 我要住**在**一间单人房

e. 我每个**周**末去公园

7. Draw a line in between each word

a. 我/喜欢/打篮球   b. 我/周末/总是/和/朋友/一起/踢足球   c. 有空/的时候/我/喜欢/玩/电脑

d. 我/暑假/的时候/想/去/德国/度假   e. 我/爸爸妈妈/要/住在/一间/双人房

f. 早上/我/去/海边　g．我/星期六/打算/去/公园/跑步

8. Spot the translation mistakes and correct them

a. 我晚上十点睡觉: I go to bed at ~~10am~~ **10pm**

b. 我非常喜欢打篮球: I ~~hate~~ **really like** playing basketball

c. 我不要去海边: I ~~am going~~ **don't want** to go to the seaside

d. 我要做很多作业: I am ~~not~~ **going to** to do ~~any~~ **lots of** homework

e. 我想跑步: I ~~am going~~ **would like** to run

f. 我打算坐火车去: I am ~~going~~ **planning** to travel by ~~plane~~ **train**

g. 我打算住在一间双人房: I am planning to stay in a ~~single~~ **double** room

9. Translate into English:

a. I go by plane　b. I am going to go　c. I am planning to stay in　d. I would like to go the toilet

e. I watch movies in the living room　f. My bedroom is big　g. I eat vegetables for dinner

h. I have eggs for breakfast　i. I don't make dinner　j. I work on the computer

10. Translate into Chinese

a. 我早上七点起床。七点二十五分左右我吃早饭　b. 我星期六要去中国

c. 我每天都在卧室里玩电脑　d. 我从来不打篮球　e. 我每天早上六点半起床

f. 我早饭吃很多　g. 我要坐船去法国　h. 有空的时候，我踢足球和看书

i. 无聊的时候，我常常上网

11. Write in Pinyin

a. chī / **wǎn/ fàn**　b. wǒ / **kàn**　c. wǒ / **zuò**　d. wǒ / **hē**　e. wǒ / **yǒu**　f. wǒ / **gōngzuò**　g. wǒ /**xiūxi**

h. wǒ / **shuìjiào**　i. wǒ /**wán**

Question Skills 4: Daily routine/House/Home life/Holidays (Page 220)

1. Complete the questions with the correct option

a. 你和**谁**去海边？　b. 周末的时候你喜欢做**什么**？　c. 她**怎么**去学校？　d. 他**几**点吃早饭？

e. 你觉得山区**怎么样**？　f. 她**什么时候**要去北京？

2. Complete the characters

a. what - 什么　b. what is it like - 怎么**样**　c. what time - 几**点**　d. when - 十么**时候**　e. where - **哪**儿

f. how - **怎么**

3. Match each statement below to one of the questions included in activity 1 above

a. 他早上七点半吃早饭 – **D**　b. 她八月的时候要去北京 – **F**　c. 山区非常美，我很喜欢 – **E**

d. 她坐公共汽车 – **C**　e. 我喜欢踢足球和跑步 – **B**　f. 我的男朋友一起去 - **A**

4. Translate into Chinese

a. 谁？　b. 什么时候？　c. 和谁？　d. 几点？　e. 怎么样？　f. 在哪儿？　g. 为什么？

5. Translate into Chinese

a. 你喜欢喝什么？ b. 你几点看电视？   c. 有空的时候，你做什么？ d. 你为什么喜欢中国？

e. 你和谁去电影院？ f. 你什么时候去法国度假？   g. 你在哪儿踢足球？

6. Split questions

他怎**么去中国？**   你和**谁一起去公园？**   她什么**时候想去爬山？**   你喜欢吃**什么？**

他们几**点去打球？**   他在**哪儿看书？**   你觉得美国**怎么样？**   你们怎**么去城市？**

你为什么**喜欢游泳？**

VOCABULARY TESTS

Unit 1: "Talking about my age" TOTAL SCORE: /30 (Page 222)

1a. Translate the following (worth one point each) into Chinese

I am called… – 我叫

My big brother – 我哥哥

I am ten years old – 我十岁。

I am six years old – 我六岁。

I am seven years old – 我七岁。

I am eight years old – 我八岁。

I am nine years old – 我九岁。

I am eleven years old – 我十一岁。

I am twelve years old – 我十二岁。

I am thirteen years old – 我十三岁。

1b. Translate the following (worth two points each) into Chinese

My big sister – 我姐姐

My little sister is called – 我妹妹叫

I am called Jean. – 我叫 Jean。

He is fifteen years old – 他十五岁。

She is fourteen years old – 她十四岁。

He is sixteen years old - 她十六岁。

My little sister is four years old – 我妹妹四岁。

My little brother is five years old – 我弟弟五岁。

He is called… – 他叫

She is called… – 她叫

Unit 2: "Saying when my birthday is" TOTAL SCORE: /30 (Page 223)

1a. Translate the following (worth one point each) into Chinese

My name is… - 我叫

I am ten years old – 我十岁。

My friend is called Frank – 我的朋友叫 **Frank**。

He is eighteen years old - 他十八岁。

3rd May – 五月三日

4th April – 四月四日

5th June – 六月五日

6th September – 九月六日

10th October - 十月十日

8th July – 七月八日

1b. Translate the following (worth one point each) into Chinese

I am 17. My birthday is on 21st June. – 我十七岁。我的生日是六月二十一日。

My friend is called John. He is 19 years old. – 我的朋友叫 **John**。他十九岁。

My big sister is called Ru. She is 22 years old. – 我姐姐叫 **Ru**。她二十二岁。

My birthday is on 27th July. – 我的生日是七月二十七日。

My little brother's birthday is on 23rd March. – 我弟弟的生日是三月二十三日。

My name is Li. I am 18. My birthday is on 30th June. – 我叫 **Li**。我十八岁。我的生日是六月三十日。

My name is Fei Li. I am 26 years old. – 我叫 **Fei Li**。我二十六岁。

He is Chinese. – 他是中国人。

My little brother is called Robert. His birthday is on 31st January. – 我弟弟叫 **Robert.**他的生日是一月三十一日。

I am British. My birthday is 2nd December. – 我是英国人。我的生日是十二月二日。

Unit 3: "Describing hair and eyes" TOTAL SCORE: /30 (Page 224)

1a. Translate the following (worth one point each) into Chinese

He is called Joshua. – 他叫 Joshua。

She is sixteen years old. – 她十六岁。

I have – 我有

She doesn't have – 她没有

Hair – 头发

Eyes – 眼睛

I have white hair – 我有白色的头发。

She has red hair – 她有红色的头发。

He doesn't have black eyes – 他没有黑色的眼睛。

He doesn't have hair – 他没有黑色的头发。

1b. Translate the following (worth two points each) into Chinese

She has red hair – 她有红色的头发。

I have black hair – 我有黑色的头发。

He doesn't have blond hair – 他没有金色的头发。

I have brown hair. I don't have brown eyes – 我有棕色的头发。我没有棕色的眼睛。

I am 16 years old. I don't have black hair – 我十六岁。我没有黑色的头发。

She is called Misha. She doesn't have white hair. – 她叫 Misha。她没有白色的头发。

My brother doesn't have blond hair – 我哥哥没有金色的头发。

My friend is 22 years old, her birthday is 8th February. – 我的朋友二十二岁，她的生日是二月八日。

He doesn't have hair. – 他没有头发。

My big sister has black hair, not brown hair. – 我姐姐有黑色的头发，没有棕色的头发。

Unit 4 "Talking about my family/numbers 1-100" TOTAL SCORE: /30 (Page 225)

1a. Translate the following (worth one point each) into Chinese

My little brother – 我弟弟

My big brother – 我哥哥

My big sister – 我姐姐

My little sister – 我妹妹

My dad – 我爸爸

My mum – 我妈妈

My grandfather – 我爷爷

My grandmother – 我奶奶

I have two little brothers – 我有两个弟弟。

Five people – 五个人

1b. Translate the following (worth two points each) into Chinese

I have two little brothers. – 我有两个弟弟。

My father, mother and two big brothers. – 我爸爸、妈妈和两个哥哥。

My relationship with my little brother is not good. – 我和弟弟关系不好。

My grandma is 100 years old. – 我奶奶一百岁。

I have 3 big sisters. – 我有三个姐姐。

He is 78 years old. – 他七十八岁。

She is 67 years old. – 她六十七岁。

My father is 54 years old. – 我爸爸五十四岁。

My mother is 44 years old. – 我妈妈四十四岁。

I don't have a little sister. – 我没有妹妹 。

Unit 5 "Saying where I live and am from" TOTAL SCORE: /30 (Page 226)
1a. Translate the following (worth one point each) into Chinese

My name is An. – 我叫 An。

I live in – 我住在

I live in the South of China. – 我住在中国的南部。

I am Chinese. - 我是中国人。

She lives in the west of the UK. – 她住在英国的西部。

She is not British. – 她不是英国人。

He lives in China. – 他住在中国。

My friend and I live in the north of the US. – 我和我的朋友住在美国的北部。

I am American. – 我是美国人。

His grandma lives in South Africa. – 他奶奶住在南非。

1b. Translate the following sentences (worth two points each) into Chinese

My older brother is called Jason. – 我哥哥叫 Jason。

My younger sister is called Gemma. – 我妹妹叫 Gemma。

I live in China. – 我住在中国。

She lives in the UK. – 她住在英国。

He is not British. – 他不是英国人。

She lives in the western part of the US. – 她住在美国的西部。

I am British. I live in the centre of China. – 我是英国人。我住在中国的中部。

I am 15 years old. I am Chinese. – 我十五岁。我是中国人。

I am Chinese. I live in the eastern part of the US. – 我是中国人。我住在美国的东部。

He is American. He lives in the UK. – 他是美国人。他住在英国。

Unit 6 "Describing myself and my family members" TOTAL SCORE: /30 (Page 227)

1a. Translate the following (worth one point each) into Chinese

Very tall – 很高

Bad – 坏

Ugly - 丑

Good-looking – 好看

Generous – 大方

Fun – 好玩

Slim – 苗条

Very cute – 很可爱

Fat – 胖

1b. Translate the following (worth two points each) into Chinese

My mother is a little bit mean. - 我妈妈有一点小气。

Because my father is very generous. – 因为我爸爸很大方。

My older sister is beautiful. - 我姐姐很美。

My younger sister is cute. – 我妹妹很可爱。

There are five people in my family. – 我家有五个人。

I get along with big sister because she is fun. – 我和姐姐关系好，因为她很好玩。

My relationship with my little sister is not good. – 我和妹妹关系不好。

I like my grandfather because he is very generous. – 我喜欢我爷爷，因为他很大方。

My grandmother is eighty five years old. - 我奶奶八十五岁。

I have a good relationship with her. – 我和她关系好。

Unit 7 "Talking about pets" TOTAL SCORE: /40 (Page 228)

1a. Translate the following (worth one point each) into Chinese

A dog - 一只狗

Two birds - 两只鸟

Six cats – 六只猫

Four small birds – 四只小鸟

Five fish – 五条鱼

Three snakes – 三条蛇

Two small cats – 两只小猫

It is extremely cute. – 它非常可爱。

It is not ugly. – 它不丑。

1b. Translate the following (worth three points each) into Chinese

I would like to have a dog. – 我想要一只狗。

I have two small cats. – 我有两只小猫。

At home I have two small fish. – 我家有两条小鱼。

My big sister has a big cat and a small dog. – 我姐姐有一只大猫和一只小狗。

I don't have any birds. - 我没有鸟。

My friend would like to have a bird. – 我的朋友想要一只鸟。

It is extremely fat. – 它非常胖。

I wouldn't like to have a snake. – 我想要一条蛇。

I have a dog, it is very fun. – 我有一只狗，它很好玩。

My bird is not cute. – 我的鸟不可爱。

Unit 8 "Talking about jobs" TOTAL SCORE: /40 (Page 229)

1a. Translate the following (worth one point each) into Chinese

He is a worker. – 他是工人。

He is a nurse. – 他是护士。

She is a doctor. – 她是医生。

She works in a company. – 她在公司工作。

She likes this job. – 她喜欢这个工作。

Because it is very interesting. – 因为很有意思。

He doesn't like this job. - 他不喜欢这个工作。

She is an artist. – 她是画家。

He is an engineer. – 他是工程师。

She works at home. – 她在家工作。

1b. Translate the following sentences (worth three points each) into Chinese

My dad is a teacher. – 我爸爸是老师。

My mother is a nurse. – 我妈妈是护士。

She works in a hospital. – 我妈妈在医院工作。

They like this job but think it's hard. – 他们喜欢这个工作，可是觉得很难。

He likes this job because... – 他喜欢这个工作因为…

She likes this job because it is easy. – 她喜欢这个工作，因为很容易。

My grandad works in a company. – 我爷爷在公司工作。

He is a teacher, he works in a school. – 他是老师。他在学校工作。

He doesn't like this job because it is stressful. – 他不喜欢这个工作，因为很有压力。

He likes this job but thinks its tiring. – 他喜欢这个工作，但是觉得很累。

UNIT 9 "Comparing people" TOTAL SCORE: /50 (Page 230)

1a. Translate the following (worth two points each) into Chinese

Your daughter is taller than me. – 你女儿比我高。

He is more generous than her. – 他比她大方。

His son is not as fat as him. – 他儿子没有他胖。

She is slimmer than her. – 她比她苗条。

Her boyfriend is better looking than me. – 她男朋友比我好看。

My girlfriend is happier than me. – 我女朋友比我高兴。

I am not as busy as him. – 我没有他忙。

My dog is as big as yours. – 我的狗和你的一样大。

My bird is not as old as your cat. – 我的鸟没有你的猫老。

She is as good looking as me. – 她和我一样好看。

1b. Translate the following (worth 3 points each) into Chinese

My son is fatter than me. – 我儿子比我胖。

My daughter is slimmer than me. – 我女儿比我苗条。

My big brother is not as handsome as your big brother. – 我哥哥没有你哥哥帅。

My grandson is friendlier than my daughter. – 我孙子比我女儿友好。

My little sister and I are taller than my mother. – 我和妹妹比妈妈高。

My grandfather is not as ugly as my grandmother. – 我爷爷没有我奶奶难看。

My cat is not as good as my dog. – 我的猫没有我的狗好。

My fish is as fun as my grandma. – 我的鱼和我奶奶一样好玩。

Unit 10 "Talking about what is in my schoolbag" TOTAL SCORE: /40   (Page 231)

1a. Translate the following (worth one point each) into Chinese

I have a pen. – 我有一支笔。

I have a ruler. – 我有一把尺子。

I have three pens. - 我有三支笔。

In the schoolbag, there is/are... – 书包里有…

I have lots of things. – 我有很多东西。

My friend has... – 我的朋友有…

I don't have... – 我没有…

I have some books. – 我有一些书。

In the schoolbag, there are five books. – 我书包里有五本书。

In the schoolbag, there aren't any pens. – 我书包里没有笔。

1b. Translate the following (worth three points each) into Chinese

In the schoolbag, there are four books. – 书包里有四本书。

My friend has a pen and a ruler. – 我的朋友有一支笔和一把尺子。

I have a schoolbag and a book. - 我有一个书包和一本书。

I don't have a pen. – 我没有笔。

There are lots of students in the classroom. – 教室里有很多学生。

My friend has a Chinese writing brush. – 我的朋友有一支毛笔。

I have a pen and two books. – 我有一支笔和两本书。

Many schoolbags. – 很多书包。

20 tables and 5 chairs. – 二十张桌子和五把椅子。

In the schoolbag, there are some rulers. - 书包里有一些尺子。

Unit 11 & 12 "Talking about food" TOTAL SCORE: /80 (Page 232)
1a. Translate the following (worth three points each) into Chinese

I like to drink water. – 我喜欢喝水。

I love to eat bread. – 我喜欢吃面包。

I don't like fish that much. – 我不太喜欢吃鱼。

I really don't like to eat meat. – 我非常不喜欢吃肉。

Because fruit is very tasty. – 因为水果很好吃。

Because vegetables are delicious. – 因为青菜很好吃。

I prefer to drink tea. – 我更喜欢喝茶。

Milk is not nice to drink. – 牛奶不好喝。

I love to eat noodles. – 我爱吃面条。

I like to eat rice the most. – 我最喜欢吃米饭。

1b. Translate the following (worth five points each) into Chinese

I love rice because it is delicious. – 我爱吃米饭，因为很好吃。

I like soup the most. – 我最喜欢喝汤。

I really like to eat lamb for dinner. – 我晚饭非常喜欢吃羊肉。

I prefer to eat bread for breakfast. – 我早饭更喜欢吃面包。

I love fish and noodles. - 我爱吃鱼和面条。

I don't like vegetables. – 我不喜欢吃青菜。

I don't drink tea at lunch. – 我午饭不喝茶。

I like to eat rice and vegetables. – 我喜欢吃米饭和青菜。

I like pork because it is delicious. – 我喜欢猪肉，因为好吃。

Chicken is tastier than fish. – 鸡肉比鱼好吃。

Unit 13 "Describing clothes and accessories" TOTAL SCORE: /50 (Page 233)

1a. Translate the following (worth two points each) into Chinese

When it is hot – 天气热的时候

When it is cold – 天气冷的时候

Mum likes to wear white jackets. – 妈妈喜欢穿白色的大衣/夹克。

I sometimes wear black socks. – 我有时候穿黑色的袜子。

I always wear red jumpers. – 我总是穿红色的毛衣。

I rarely wear hats. – 我很少戴帽子。

Some brown shirts. – 一些棕色的衬衣。

I like to wear blue socks. – 我喜欢穿蓝色的袜子。

Black shoes. – 黑色的鞋子。

1b. Translate the (worth three points each) into Chinese

I often wear a black hat. – 我常常戴黑色的帽子。

When at home, I wear a jumper. – 在家的时候，我常常穿毛衣。

When at school, we wear a white shirt. – 在学校的时候，我们穿白色的衬衣。

My mum wears trousers. – 我妈妈穿裤子。

My grandma always wear a watch. – 我奶奶总是戴手表。

My friend likes to wear high heel shoes. – 我的朋友喜欢穿高跟鞋。

When the weather is cold, I wear a jacket. – 天气冷的时候，我穿大衣/夹克。

When hanging out with my friends... - 和朋友出去玩的时候...

I rarely wear a belt. - 我很少系皮带。

Unit 14 "Talking about free time" TOTAL SCORE: /70 (Page 234)

1a. Translate the following (worth two points each) into Chinese

Everyday – 每天

I often – 我常常/经常

I don't like to watch TV – 我看电视。

I like to play ball games – 我打球。

Sometimes, my dad and I... – 有时候，我和爸爸...

When the weather is good – 天气好的时候

Every week, my friend and I... – 每个星期，我和我的朋友...

I play on my computer. – 我玩电脑。

Read books with me – 和我一起看书。

I read novels. – 我看小说。

1b. Translate the following (worth five points each) into Chinese

I rarely play basketball – 我很少打篮球。

I often go to my friend's house to play. – 我常常去我朋友家玩。

Sometimes dad and I watch TV together. – 有时候，我和爸爸一起看电视。

My little brother and I play ball games everyday. – 我弟弟和我每天都打球。

I have breakfast everyday. – 我每天都吃早饭。

When the weather is nice, we play basketball. – 天气好的时候，我们打篮球。

When the weather is bad, I watch movies. – 天气不好的时候，我看电影。

My dad reads books at the weekend. – 我爸爸周末看书。

My younger brothers and I watch TV together. – 我和弟弟一起看电视。

Sometimes my friend and I have lunch together. – 有时候，我和朋友一起吃午饭。

Unit 15 "Talking about weather and free time" TOTAL SCORE: /60 (Page 235)

1a. Translate the following (worth two points each) into Chinese

When the weather is good – 天气好的时候

When the weather is bad – 天气不好的时候

When it is sunny – 晴天的时候

When it is cold – 天气冷的时候

When it is hot – 天气热的时候

When I have free time – 我有空的时候

When I hang out with friends – 我和朋友出去玩的时候

I go to the seaside – 我去海边

I go to the mountains – 我去山区

I go to the park – 我去公园

1b. Translate the following (worth four points each) into Chinese

When the weather is good, I go to the seaside. – 天气好的时候，我去海边。

When it rains, we go to the cinema to watch a movie. – 下雨的时候，我们电影院看电影。

At the weekend, I play on the computer. – 周末的时候，我玩电脑。

When it is hot, she goes to the seaside or the park. – 天气热的时候，她去海边或者去公园。

When I have free time, I listen to music. – 有空的时候，我听音乐。

When it is cloudy, I watch TV with dad at home. – 多云的时候，我和爸爸在家看电视。

When it is sunny, they go to the mountains. – 晴天的时候，他们去山区。

When it snows, my girlfriend and I go skiing in the mountains. – 下雪的时候，我和我的女朋友一起去山区滑雪。

We go to my friend's house to listen to music. - 我们去朋友家听音乐。

When the sky is clear, my dad and I go fishing by the lake. – 天蓝的时候，我和爸爸去湖边钓鱼。

Unit 16 "Talking about my daily routine" TOTAL SCORE: /40 (Page 236)

1a. Translate the following (worth one point each) into Chinese

I get up – 我起床

I have breakfast – 我吃早饭

In the early morning – 早上

In the late morning – 上午

Every evening – 每天晚上（都）

Around six o'clock – 六点左右

I go home – 我回家

At noon – 中午

At 11.25am – 上午十一点二十五分

At 9.50pm or so – 晚上九点五十分左右

1b. Translate the following (worth three points each) into Chinese

Around 7.00 in the morning, I have breakfast. – 早上七点左右，我吃早点。

I often wash my hands. – 我常常洗手

I have lunch. – 我吃午饭。

Around 8 o'clock in the evening, I have dinner. – 晚上八点左右，我吃晚饭。

I go to school by bus. – 我坐公共汽车去学校。

I like to watch television in the evening. – 我晚上喜欢看电视。

I go back home at 4.30pm. – 我四点半回家。

Around 6pm, I play on the computer – 晚上六点，我玩电脑。

I go to bed at around 11.30pm. – 我晚上十一点半左右睡觉。

Every evening at around 9.55 – 每天晚上九点五十五分左右

Unit 17 "Describing my house" TOTAL SCORE: /40 (Page 237)
1a. Translate the following (worth one point each) into Chinese

I live in – 我住在

In the mountains – 在山区

An interesting city – 一个有意思的城市

In the boring countryside – 在没意思的农村

My house is big – 我的房子很大。

At the beautiful seaside – 在海边

In the dining room – 在饭厅里

In my bedroom – 在我的卧室里

The living room is extremely small. – 客厅非常小。

My house is quite old. – 我的房子比较老。

1b. Translate the following (worth three points each) into Chinese

My house has four bedrooms. – 我的房子有四个房间。

I like our living room the most. – 我最喜欢我们的客厅。

I often play on my phone in the study. – 我经常在书房里玩手机。

My house has two bathrooms. – 我的房子有两个浴室。

My older sister's house is really big. – 我姐姐的房子非常大。

My friend's house is a little bit small. – 我朋友的房子有一点小。

We live at the seaside. – 我们住在海边。

My friend lives in the city. – 我的朋友住在城市。

My grandma lives in the mountains. – 我奶奶住在山区。

I sometimes listen to music in the garden. – 我有时候在花园里听音乐。

Unit 18 "Talking about my home life" TOTAL SCORE: /40 (Page 238)

1a. Translate the following (worth one point each) into Chinese

I chat with mum everyday. – 我每天都和妈妈聊天。

I often go on the internet. – 我经常上网。

I sometimes do homework in my bedroom. – 我有时候在卧室里做作业。

I never read comics. – 我从来不看漫画书。

I usually watch films in the living room. – 我一般在客厅里看电影。

I always listen to music in the dining room. – 我总是在客厅里听音乐。

I have a rest at around 6pm. – 我晚上六点左右作业休息。

I get dressed at around 7am. – 我早上七点左右穿好衣服。

I play on my phone in the toilet. – 我在厕所里玩手机。

I make food in the kitchen. – 我在厨房里做饭。

1b. Translate the following (worth three points each) into Chinese

Everyday I have breakfast in the kitchen. – 我每天都在厨房里吃早饭。

I rarely go on the internet. – 我很少上网。

It says on TV that the weather is cloudy today. – 电脑上说今天天气多云。

There are some books under the table. – 桌子下有一些书。

Everyday I watch TV series in the living room. – 我每天都在客厅里看电视剧。

I sometimes have lunch in the study. – 我有时候在书房里吃午饭。

I usually rest in the garden. – 我一般在花园里休息。

I usually play on the computer with my little brother in the living room. – 我一般在客厅里跟我弟弟玩电脑。

I always read comics in the bathroom. – 我总是在浴室里看漫画书。

When I have free time, I watch a movie. – 我有空的时候看电影。

Unit 19 "My Holiday plans" TOTAL SCORE: /70 (Page 239)

1a. Translate the following (worth two points each) into Chinese

To have a holiday – 度假

We are going to – 我们要

My family and I are going to – 我和家人要

I am going to take photos everyday – 我每天都要拍照。

We are planning to – 我们打算

I would like to – 我想

I am planning to take a boat to – 我打算坐船去

I am going to the French seaside. – 我要去法国的海边。

I think it should be fun. – 我觉得应该会很好玩。

I am going to China by plane. – 我要坐飞机去中国。

1b. Translate the following (worth five points each) into Chinese

I think it is sure to be extremely good. – 我觉得一定会非常好。

I am going by train to the British countryside. – 我要坐火车去英国的农村。

We are going to France to have a holiday. – 我们要去法国度假。

I am going to spend two weeks there with my family. – 我和家人要在那儿住两个星期。

We are going to go on holiday to China tomorrow. – 我们明天要去中国度假。

We are going to stay in the US for two weeks. We are going by plane. – 我们要在美国住两个星期。我们坐飞机去。

My friend and I are planning to stay there for 3 weeks. – 我和我的朋友打算在那儿住三个星期。

We are going to the city by car. – 我们要开车去城市。

Mum and dad are planning to stay in a double room. – 爸爸妈妈打算住在一个双人房。

I think it might be boring. – 我觉得可能会很无聊。